THE MILFORD SERIES
Popular Writers of Today

Volume Fifteen

Lightning from a Clear Sky

Tolkien,
The Trilogy,
and
The Silmarillion

Richard Mathews

R. REGINALD

THE *Borgo Press*

SAN BERNARDINO, CALIFORNIA

MCMLXXVIII

To Julie

Library of Congress Cataloging in Publication Data:

Lightning from a clear sky.

(The Milford Series) (Popular Writers of Today; v. 15)
Bibliography: pp. 62-63
1.   Tolkien, John Ronald Reuel, 1892-1973—Criticism and
interpretation. I. Title.
PR6039.O32Z695   823'.9'12   78-922
ISBN 0-89370-221-8

Produced, designed, and published by R. Reginald, The Borgo Press,
P.O. Box 2845, San Bernardino, CA 92406. Composition by Mary A.
Burgess. Cover design by Judy Cloyd.

First Edition————July, 1978

Preface

John Ronald Reuel Tolkien has illuminated the imaginative vision of millions of readers. When C. S. Lewis described that illumination as being "like lightning from a clear sky," he chose an apt expression. Lightning is a transcendent and mysterious phenomenon in which we recognize force, mystery, sublime power, and a cleanly striking beauty. It has traditionally been a symbol for the highest creativity and has often been linked to spiritual illumination. Lightning's sudden electrifying clarity momentarily transforms the world, and its force has moved both the heart and intelligence of man. It is a message from the heavens, visible evidence of lofty powers beyond man's understanding or control.

Lightning is an appropriate metaphor for the surreal precision and the spiritual power of Tolkien's fiction. It is an ancient symbol, a power recognized and mythologized by primitive peoples and intellectuals alike, and serves well to indicate the startling mythic vision of Tolkien, an imaginative approach nearly lost to man in the technological age. Tolkien has introduced millions of readers in contemporary culture to possibilities and challenges found in ancient and scriptural literature. His narratives re-mytholgize our overly rational world, placing moral force over individual psychology and symbolic over realistic quest. Tolkien has brought to life in modern English an epic and heroic view of the world similar to that found in *Beowulf*, *Sir Gawain and the Green Knight*, and the Northern epics and sagas. Insights and values are *embodied* in characters and worked out in quests and battles of great heroes with a scope and range far greater than that allowed by the problem-ridden psychologizing of realistic and conventional fiction.

It has puzzled many critics that Tolkien should be so popular in America—perhaps more popular here, in fact, than in his own country—especially since his epic antecedents are English and Northern rather than American. In a country where millions visit Disneyland or Disneyworld, this should be understandable. Both parks were built on the foundation of America's most appealing folk tradition: the tall tale. Many of the quests, virtues, and impulses of the medieval epics are reenacted in American pioneer and cowboy folk history. These popular stories cultivated a taste for just the sort of fiction Tolkien wanted to write. Edgar Allan Poe provided the American imagination with compelling fantasies of horror, guilt and revenge, sinister forces as frightening as anything in Mordor. Ian M. Slater recently pointed out in *Fantasiae*, the newsletter of the Fantasy Association, that Longfellow's America Indian epic *Hiawatha* was based partly on one of Tolkien's major influences, *The Kalevala* of Finland. The American sensibility, to a greater extent than that of any other modern civilized nation, was formed from the same materials which molded sensibilities of saga man.

Tolkien succeeded in America because he depends upon the reader's imagination rather than an assumed level of philosophical and literary erudition for entrance into his fictive world. Existential philosophy, absurdist techniques borrowed from France and Germany, and a host of cerebral-linguistic games dominate much of twentieth century fiction, a literature which seems to be written for an upperclass educational elite, out of touch with fundamental

American instincts and realities. Tolkien's heroic idealism speaks more to the point. Not that he fails to bring deep learning to his writing, but he reaches a broader audience, a cross-section as diverse as that reached by the bards and minstrels who recited tales aloud in ancient days. Tolkien thought of himself as an ordinary man, and chose to build his fantasy fiction upon a familiar base of common experience. By introducing elemental heroism and grandeur into his writing, he heightened the possibilities of the ordinary or commonplace so that each reader could come to share an experience of transcendence. Tolkien was investigating an imaginative process which once had filled the world with the living literature of myth. If, as many people complain, the contemporary age has no myths, Tolkien's criticism and novels demonstrate for children and for adults alike that myth is alive and well in a hole in the ground, dwarfed perhaps for the moment, but eager to grow strong and vigorous again.

The disappearance of myth coincides with the decline of religious belief, and Tolkien felt both of these losses deeply. In fact, the great theme in his writing is loss; his characters are largely thieves who perpetuate cycles of loss by continuing to take and retake possessions—thrones, trinkets, lands, people. Tolkien as a Christian writer sees sacrifice and voluntary loss of another kind as necessary to break the cycle. The ultimate task is not to steal power from the gods, but to relinquish and destroy the threat of that power forever. In the process one may lose the possibility of employing this power for good, but the cause, Tolkien shows, is far greater than these relatively inconsequential sacrifices. Only by giving up the possession of power will the soul be preserved.

In this sense, Tolkien's work is the most important story we can read in our time, for it offers us both a challenge and a path. The path lies in the direction of rich mythic imagination—Tolkien calls it subcreation. Its significance is that it proceeds not by stealing and possessiveness, but by creative giving in harmonious accord with God's Creation. Tolkien clearly recognizes that man's will, despite his best intentions, is weak. Though he tries to pattern himself after his Creator, he always seems to fall away from his good intentions. Man steals the apple, and Tolkien's diminutive hobbits appear to be irredeemable thieves themselves. Tolkien shows us how to move from thief to subcreator—the path, essentially, which both Bilbo and Frodo pursue. Our difficult challenge is to give up the materialism to which we are so uncomfortably wed—and annihilate the frightening Power of ultimate weaponry. In the process, we may have to fight a war as large as that which shakes the universe of Middle Earth before we see the depth of our need. If it comes to that, let us hope we have both a Gandalf and a hobbit, a fount of ancient knowledge and a humble heart, to face it and prevail.

Richard Mathews
Gulfport, Florida
June, 1978

I. J. R. R. TOLKIEN

The literary creations of J. R. R. Tolkien are inextricably bound up with a rich and original family life. While he was prompted to write partly because of his academic interests in philology, his love of literature, and because of the experience of the horrifying world war he was part of, the liveliness and sensitivity of his fiction owes a great deal to his wife and children, and to his own upbringing as well. He was born in Bloemfontein, South Africa, where his father worked for the Bank of Africa. He returned to England with his mother for a visit when he was three, and while they were away Tolkien's father became ill and died. Mabel Tolkien remained in England with her two sons, and Tolkien never returned to Africa. The element of sudden deep personal loss young Tolkien felt at his father's death must have deepened when eight years later his mother, then 34, was found to have diabetes, and died shortly after the illness was detected. The boys were looked after by their mother's priest, Father Francis Morgan, and by an aunt, but Tolkien was an orphan before he was a teenager. His childhood was deeply impressed with the marks of love, and the feelings of loss which followed the early death of his parents.

Father Morgan valued education, and it became the approved path for the young boy. "Ronald" completed his schooling on scholarship at King Edward's with the goal of working for a scholarship at Oxford. Most importantly, he fell in love. At the tender age of fifteen, he found himself in love with Edith Bratt, an orphan whom he had met a year earlier. Father Morgan disapproved of Edith, and Tolkien was forbidden to see her, but in 1910, when Tolkien won a place at Exeter College, Oxford University, he was still meeting Edith, and on his 21st birthday he was free to court and marry her. They were formally engaged in 1914, on the eve of the outbreak of the war. After earning an honors degree at Oxford, he was commissioned to the 11th Lancashire Fusiliers, and he and Edith were married in March, 1916, just before he travelled to France on active duty as a second lieutenant Battalion Signalling Officer. Less than a year later he was back from the front, in a hospital with "trench fever," and there, while recuperating, he began writing "The Book of Lost Tales," a collection of original legends which eventually became *The Silmarillion*.

Tolkien's first son John was born in 1917. Tolkien was then 25 years old, with more military duty to survive before the end of the war. Fortunately, Armistice was only a year away. The war over, he returned to Oxford with his family and joined the staff working to complete the great *Oxford English Dictionary*. It was an academic job perfectly suited to his interests in literature, linguistics, and philology. After some highly respected work there, he was offered a teaching position at the Leeds University (where his second son, Michael, was born) and he completed his first major scholarly undertaking, a new edition of *Sir Gawain and the Green Knight*, with E. V. Gordon. When the work was published in 1925, Tolkien, then 33, was elected Rawlinson and Bosworth Professor of Anglo-Saxon at Oxford University.

The legends of "The Book of Lost Tales" were for Tolkien largely a private exercise of narrative invention; but the deep experiences underlying the tales he shared only with his wife Edith. Tolkien's biographer, Humphrey Carpenter, explains that "Of all his legends, the tale of Beren and Luthien was the one most loved by Tolkien." This story, Tolkien's first creative work of genius, is now available in the posthumously published *Silmarillion*. Carpenter reports that Edith used to dance for Tolkien in the woods, and that this was the inspiration for his story of the mortal Beren who loved an immortal elven maiden Luthien Tinuviel. In the love of Beren and Luthien, the loss of the Silmarils is partly compensated, just as Tolkien's marriage to Edith and the close family life they shared compensated for their own orphan backgrounds.

If Edith was the inspiration for his adult writing, his children inspired him in another direction—a charming simplicity in a warm and humorous writing style. Tolkien's capabilities for storytelling were thoroughly exercised in *The Father Christmas Letters* which he wrote and illustrated for his children each year starting in 1920. Inscribed in a shivery hand, the letters from Father Christmas told of funny and convincing adventures involving the North Polar Bear, Snow-elves, Red Gnomes, Cave-bears, and the Polar Bear's nephews, Paksu and Valkotukka. Father Christmas eventually took on as secretary an Elf named Ilbereth, a name quite similar to Elbereth, "Star-Queen" in Sindarin language, the lady known to the High-elves as Varda, ruler of the Firmament and, like the Catholic Mary, a mediatrix. Tolkien's linguistic inventiveness and his mythic imagination were thus exercised in his writing for his children, much in the same way his love for his wife was expressed in the "Beren and Luthien" story.

Family lore became Tolkien's uniquely personal vehicle for myth-making. He made up stories for all sorts of special occasions. Humphrey Carpenter mentions "the irrepressible villain 'Bill Stickers,' a huge bulk of a man who always got away with everything. His name was taken from a notice on an Oxford gate that said BILL STICKERS WILL BE PROSECUTED, and a similar source provided the name of the righteous person who was always in pursuit of Stickers, 'Major Road Ahead.' " Carpenter explains that the stories began when his eldest son, John could not get to sleep. "Tolkien would sit beside him on the bed and tell him stories about 'Carrots,' a boy with red hair who climbed into a cuckoo clock and went off on a series of strange adventures." To a large extent the family myths centered around made-up words and funny names—the North Polar Bear and Bill Stickers are only two examples—and Tolkien's storytelling became a way of sharing his professional delight in words and their meanings with his family. The Father Christmas letters continued for over twenty years; John, Michael, Christopher, and Priscilla all shared in the correspondence. The healthy interaction of home and office, the elaborate investigations of scholarship combined with the simple expressions of human love secure in the family experience, contribute substantially to the appealing style of Tolkien's first novel, *The Hobbit*.

Two other major influences shaping the style and direction of Tolkien's fiction remain to be mentioned, and both of them have to do with Oxford. An early and significant literary discovery was his reading of the fantasy writings of William Morris. As a student at Oxford, Tolkien was a member of Exeter College, the college Morris had attended. In the spring of 1914, when the college awarded Tolkien the Skeats Prize for English, he used the prize money to buy books of medieval Welsh and several of Morris's works including his first fantasy novel, *The House of the Wolfings*. Carpenter notes that it was one of the few modern works Tolkien read, and that "Morris's view of literature coincided with his own." In *Wolfings* Morris had "tried to recreate the excitement he himself had found in the pages of early English and Icelandic narratives. *The House of the Wolfings* is set in a land which is threatened by an invading force of Romans. . . . Many elements in the story seem to have impressed Tolkien. Its style is highly idiosyncratic, heavily laden with archaisms and poetic inversions in an attempt to recreate the aura of ancient legend. Clearly Tolkien took note of this, and it would seem that he also appreciated another facet of the writing: Morris's aptitude, despite the vagueness of time and place in which the story is set, for describing with great precision the details of his imagined landscape. Tolkien himself was to follow Morris's example in later years." Carpenter does not develop the similarities and differences in these two great English fantasy writers, but Morris's impact on the "Lost Tales" is evident. [Volume 13 of the Milford Series, *Worlds beyond the World*, provides a good introduction to Morris's fantasy writing.]

Finally, Tolkien's holding of an important professorial chair at Oxford University was not itself without significant influence upon him and his work. In this position Tolkien kept his human involvement with constant intellectual activity. His students challenged his own continued learning, and the important friends he made in the community had an enduring impact. A year after his return to Oxford from Leeds, Tolkien met another young professor there,C. S. Lewis. It was partly through long discussions with Tolkien that Lewis was converted to Christianity about 1930, and their association was later enlarged to include the author Charles Williams, an employee at the Oxford University Press. These three men and other friends formed a group known as The Inklings, who met together informally but regularly for company, conversation, and a chance to try out manuscripts aloud prior to publication. Friends and colleagues encouraged Tolkien and made suggestions, but not even Lewis, whom Tolkien credits with convincing him that his writing "could be more than a private hobby," had much stylistic impact. This fellowship of creative colleagues served more as a catalyst than as a stylistic arbiter. When Tolkien began to write *The Hobbit*, which he read aloud to the group, he had already been compiling his "Lost Tales" intermittently over thirteen years, and he had delivered his Father Christmas letters for ten years. Both his style and his sense of audience—his family, his students, his colleagues—were already formed.

II. THE HOBBIT

Tolkien created his popular prelude to *The Lord of the Rings* by allowing Bilbo his own subtitle, "There and Back Again." The motif of cyclical return becomes an important part of the story, and important for Tolkien as well, for he returns again and again to the unified myths and stories recurring in his books. The circle is a unifying image and symbolic pattern throughout Tolkien's work, and the rings *begin* in *The Hobbit* at Bag *End*; Bilbo's last name repeats the ambiguity: Baggins. The novel starts in the Spring, in April 1341 (Shire Time) and completes a full season into the Spring just one year later when Bilbo returns. The book begins with a hole in the ground, a round hobbit-hole, with a circular door and a round knob in the middle. Tolkien tells us in the first paragraph that this is "not a nasty, dirty, wet hole, filled with the ends of worms." If we pause to consider what he writes, we may conclude that the alpha and omega of Bag End is not limited in its significance to the fact that Bilbo will make an end of that "giant worm," the dragon. The story is really about something else: "It was a hobbit-hole, and that means comfort." This is "comfort" in its most deeply rooted sense, as it came into Middle English from the Latin and Old French: "to strengthen." Various characters and circles are strengthened in the novel, from the "beautiful grey ring of smoke" which Bilbo sends forth to break and float away in the first chapter, to the unbreakable Ring of Power he is joined to at the end.

In addition to the symbolic traditions behind lightning, Lewis's description of Tolkien's writing as "lightning from a clear sky" conveys the surprising, unpredictable quality of the fiction. *The Hobbit* begins with "An Unexpected Party," and the entire adventure is as much of a surprise to Bilbo as it is to any of us. Carpenter and other critics have pointed out the similarities in personality between Bilbo and Tolkien—neither of them liked surprises very much. Shocks and surprises may be fine for larger-than-life heroes who can rise to any challenge, but part of the uniqueness of Tolkien's literary achievement comes from the diminished size and importance of his hero. The fantasy novel developed by William Morris had portrayed a fairly traditional heroic type, one unusual perhaps in his greater concern for commonwealth than for personal fame and fortune, and Frodo and Bilbo, like Morris's Thiodolf, sometimes attain this state of mind. But hobbits are much more ordinary. They are not heroically courageous by instinct, and they do give considerable thought to their own fame and well-being. Even physically, Tolkien has belittled his hobbits; to the peculiarities of the funny name and small size he adds strange little feet and hairy ankles, and a fastidiousness that is often amusing. They have the cuteness of rabbits rather than the heroic stature of titans. (In fact, the hobbit resembles Bugs Bunny perhaps more than Paul Bunyon.) The hobbits live "in a hole in the ground," as far from the lightning-riddled sky as possible. But, as we have seen, it is "a very comfortable tunnel without smoke, with panelled walls, and floors tiled and carpeted. . . ." We are back again to that word "comfort." There is a strength in this predictable and secure environment, but the hobbit, like the scholar Tolkien, instinctively yearns for not only a secure contact with Mother Earth, but an illumination from the heavens as well.

The Hobbit leads us comfortably into the path of lightning. It is a children's book, but it is widely read and enjoyed by adults as the best introduction to the world which unfolds in *Lord of the Rings*. It is a comforting story which strengthens the mind of the reader, as it strengthens the central characters of the tale, serving as preparation for extraordinary realities and struggles.

The reader is bound to be involved and reassured by the very narrative style Tolkien uses. The hobbit hole is made vivid and convincing by its ordinariness— the pegs for hats and coats, the tile and carpets, the pipe Bilbo is so fond of smoking, and even the clothes he wears. The narrator addresses the reader directly: "Well, you will see whether he gained anything in the end." Here is a narrator who takes the reader into account, relies on his ability to decide and judge, and considers the reader and author in a partner relationship as he refers to Bilbo as "*our* particular hobbit." When Gandalf assures the dwarves (and simultaneously the readers) that our hobbit is fit to be a hero ("he is one of the best, one of the best—as fierce as a dragon in a pinch"), we are taken into his confidence as he explains, "If you have ever seen a dragon in a pinch, you will realize that this was only poetical exaggeration applied to any hobbit." At the same time, however, the "poetical exaggeration" foreshadows the conclusion of the book, when Bilbo does, in his own fashion, measure up to the dragon.

Another stylistic feature introduced in the opening pages gains increasing seriousness and purpose throughout this book and in the remainder of Tolkien's writing. Startled and disturbed by the strange intrusion of Gandalf and the dwarves, Bilbo is further disoriented when they begin a rowdy clean-up of his home and suddenly burst into song: "Chip the glasses and crack the plates!/ Blunt the knives and bend the forks!/That's what Bilbo Baggins hates—" Songs and verses in Tolkien's work are compelling, and frequent. At this, the first appearance of verse in the story, it is joined to the image of lightning: "And of course they did none of these dreadful things, and everything was cleaned and put away safe as quick as lightning." Bilbo is powerless before this song, and though its thrust is comic and good-natured, the one which follows it holds a real threat to the hobbit's ordinary life: "The music began all at once, so sudden and sweet that Bilbo forgot everything else, and was swept away into dark lands under strange moons, far over The Water and very far from his hobbit-hole under The Hill." The song weaves such a spell that "As they sang the hobbit felt the love of beautiful things made by hands and by cunning and by magic moving through him, a fierce and jealous love, the desire of the hearts of dwarves." As Bilbo is led to feel the lure of the quest "far over the misty mountains," he is practically undone: "He began to feel a shriek coming up inside, and very soon it burst out like the whistle of an engine coming out of a tunnel. . . .Then he fell flat on the floor, and kept on calling out 'struck by lightning, struck by lightning!' over and over again."

Despite their willingness to suspend disbelief and to share Tolkien's world, readers usually at first feel overwhelmed like Bilbo when confronted with the unexpected danger of a dragon. We are particularly struck by such a dark and inexplicable dimension because our conventional and ordinary lives lead us to believe we are safe and far from harm. Tolkien as author must have been somewhat in Gandalf's position; when Gandalf considers the challenge of the quest, he admits he ideally would have chosen someone other than Bilbo to undertake it, "a mighty Warrior, even a Hero. I tried to find one; but warriors are busy fighting one another in distant lands, and in this neighborhood heroes are scarce, or simply not to be found." He has picked instead a tiny creature, smaller than a man, conventional and vulnerable, full of fears and habits, and able to satisfy the duties of central character not as hero or warrior, but only as a sneak-thief: "That is why I settled on *burglary*," Gandalf explains, "especially when I remembered the existence of a side-door." Tolkien introduces us to his mythology through the side-door, and in the ironic play of hobbit against human, habit against hero, Tolkien brings us sneakily into his Middle Earth.

Middle English roots abound in the language of Middle Earth, and even a cursory look at how hobbit and human interact reveals Tolkien's playful ironic sensibility at work. The hobbit himself is full of contradictions. He possesses all the refinements of civilized life, but his furry little feet and rabbit-burrow life in a hole in the ground point out how far away we are from our animal origins. The hobbit is the primary focus for the exercise of Tolkien's linguistic and literary hobby. (The word "hobby" seems related to "hobbit," and akin to the Old French *hober*, "to move (+ et).") He knew and liked Sinclair Lewis's *Babbitt*, and that title may have been partly involved in his choice of hobbit. A "hob" is "a hobgolin or elf," and is a root which seems appropriate for Middle Earth. It also is used to designate a rounded peg or pin used as a target in quoits and similar games, and this sense of center pin or target seems appropriate in the context of the story as well. The name has connections with the Middle English "hobele(n)" and High German "hoppeln" which came to designate "an awkward or difficult situation" from its original sense—to jolt. That our "Unexpected Party" involves a jolt (like lightning) neatly echoes the various implications of hob at the hub of our hobbit world. The linguistic values in the opening pages are further complicated by "burglar" ("our little Bilbo Baggins, *the* burglar, the chosen and selected burglar"). The root here is "burg" and is related to borough, a fortified city. The hobbit is only your average city dweller coming to face uncanny challenges from a mythic world he has never tangled with before. That he lives in a kind of burrow adds another playful association.

Tolkien's linguistic training runs wrinkling through these stories. He had earned a considerable academic reputation while helping complete the *Oxford English Dictionary*. Though the A-H section, including both "burglar" and "hobby-hobbler-hobgoblin-hob" had been published in 1900, the later entries in the "w's" on which Tolkien worked show him to have been thoroughly proficient at the task and familiar with the backgrounds of language. Even the name "hobbit" is connected to the role of "burglar" according to the *Oxford English Dictionary*, since "Hob" is a shortened form of the Christian name Robert or Robin (Rob=Hob), formerly "a generic name for a rustic, a clown." Tolkien uses all the various senses of this name, making Bilbo and later Frodo into rustics and clowns at times and allowing them to become a type of wise fool. And, of course, the English audience would pick up the Robin association with its rustic folk hero Robin Hood, the good robber and comic burglar.

Well, Bilbo's unexpected party closes with plans for breakfast and the practical concern of how to make places for all these 14 visitors to sleep. The details are arranged, and Bilbo sleeps fitfully until "long after the break of day," filled with "un*comfort*able dreams." He starts out the next day where he left off, for the dwarves are gone, and it only remains for him to clean up and "forget about the night before," when Gandalf appears and insists that Bilbo read the message left by the dwarves, and then meet them at 11 a.m. In a final frenzy of activity, Bilbo is driven into his adventure by his habit of punctuality. Gandalf turns his orderly life around, using his punctual compulsions to force him into action. Gandalf tells him he has "just ten minutes" to keep his appointment, and for every objection Bilbo can think of, the wizard replies, "No time for it!" Bilbo finds himself dashing to the Green Dragon Inn (Dragon-End? Where they drag Bilbo in to their adventure?), distressed because he arrives without his hat and pocket-handkerchief, and apologizing for his confusion and delay since he "didn't get your note until after 10:45 to be precise." The new rules are immediately imposed: "Don't be precise," says Dwalin, "and don't worry! You will have to manage without pocket-handkerchiefs, and a good many other things, before you get to the journey's end."

The second chapter, "Roast Mutton," is full of reversals of ordinary expectations. "Roast Mutton" itself sounds normal and civilized, a perfect English dish, but it's a title that refers to new rules. The mutton suggests "comfort" again; that which appears to strengthen or nourish in a familiar, reassuring way—"Roast Mutton"—does strengthen Bilbo, but in harder moral, spiritual, and physical ways. The mutton is being roasted by trolls, who complain, "Mutton yesterday, mutton today, and blimey, if it don't look like mutton again tomorrer. . . Never a blinking bit of manflesh. . . ." Bilbo arrives as a burglar in search of a hearty meal, but finds he is about to replace that mutton and be made up into a tasty little hobbit pie, typically English pub fare. The whole expedition is about to be destroyed because its members were led astray by their civilized taste for a proper meal. They save themselves, with an epic trick straight from the Odyssey, as Gandalf keeps the trolls arguing among themselves until the sun comes up. This second sunrise in the book concludes the first adventure: the trolls are turned to stone, "for trolls, as you probably know, must be underground before dawn, or they go back to the stuff of the mountains they are made of, and never move again."

Randel Helms, one of the most perceptive critics to write about Tolkien's fiction, discusses the mythic dimensions of *The Hobbit* in *Tolkien's World*, bluntly beginning his ironic essay "The Hobbit as Swain: A World of Myth" with the assertion that "*The Hobbit* is so frankly about growing up that there is no great discovery in translating it into analytic terms; this seems indeed the only proper exegesis of such a classic. . . " Quoting the precedent of William Empson's tongue-in-cheek analysis of *Alice in Wonderland*, Helms proceeds to give us a detailed psychoanalytical-mythopoeic reading of *The Hobbit* which, though exaggerated, contains many interesting perceptions and insights. He points out that Bag End, with its round opening, is the perfect womb symbol; that Bilbo is born out of it into the world. Later the dwarves undergo a similar birth when they are imprisoned in bags or sacks by the trolls, and Bilbo "acts as midwife" to deliver them. "Now that all the members of the quest have achieved 'birth,' " Helms explains, "they are ready for the first of a sequence of adventures that will form the backbone of *The Hobbit*: the hero must enter a dark, forbidding or forbidden place, usually through a tunnel, the entrance to which is guarded by a figure of power or terror, and bring forth persons important to the quest or an object heavy with symbolic implications." These successive experiences form, he argues, "a series of advancing initiations" through which he gains symbols of strength and power—sword and ring—in short, symbols of manhood.

While acknowledging that his analysis is something of a parody, Helms asserts that the mythic psychology of the story is there because it is part of all real myth. . . it is a quality of the mythic imagination. He concludes that "Taken in and for itself, Tolkien's children's story deserves little serious, purely literary criticism." Helms isn't clear about what he means by "purely literary criticism," but it does seem that he is unwilling to regard *The Hobbit* as a very important *Ding an sich*: "The real importance of *The Hobbit* is what its creator learned in the writing." This is sensible, but it misses the point that the creator was writing it for the very audience he speaks to so often throughout the narrative—the *you* he repeatedly reaches toward. It is not merely a question of Tolkien growing up (though certainly he did develop considerably through the writing of this book); rather, it is Tolkien exploring the level and angle from which it will be possible to lead readers into the mythic and scholarly world he knew so well. This story, aimed at this family and friends, has compelling, haunting charm. Whatever the particular age group, the mythic achievement as well as the successful style are literary elements worthy of praise. Moreover, the thematic development of "comfort," provides an intriguing and complex literary subject.

One of the questions raised by Helms involves the subtitle reference "there and back." If the hobbit hole is a womb at the beginning, is it also one at the end? Helms himself suggests the problem when he points to "a curious lack of structural coherence in his children's book." He explains that "if *The Hobbit* were to keep within the traditional structure of the quest fairy tale, the story ought to have a minor climax in the encounter with the dragon and the attainment of the Arkenstone. . . But of course the book does not end that way at all. The real climax of *The Hobbit* is not Bilbo's *finding* the Arkenstone, but his *renouncing* the Arkenstone. . . . The children's book began as a symmetrical quest-tale. . . about entering, grasping, and returning, but it grew into a story not about grasping but about renouncing." He places an "unexpected climax" to the entire tale of Middle-Earth at the finding of the ring in Gollum's cave, and finds a "symmetry of renunciation" at the beginning of *Fellowship* when Bilbo finally gives up the ring, as he gave up the Arkenstone in the earlier book.

That wonderful phrase "symmetry of renunciation" can apply equally well to *The Hobbit* by itself, for the tale begins with Bilbo renouncing his comfort, and it ends with his renouncing the very treasure he renounced his comfort to attain. Bilbo has clearly fallen within a ring of renunciation in this single book, and if Tolkien departs from the expected "structural coherence of a children's book," it is because he has, even prior to the beginning of the story, himself renounced a linear and progressive view of reality. In reply to Helms's comment that the book "deserves little serious, purely literary criticism," it's well to let Tolkien speak for himself, for although his comments are made in his famous essay on *Beowulf*, the general tenor of his remarks applies equally well to critical treatment of *The Hobbit*: "Nearly all the censure, and most of the praise, that has been bestowed on *The Beowulf* has been due either to the belief that it was something that it was *not*—for example, primitive, pagan, Teutonic, an allegory (political or mythical), or most often, an epic; or to disappointment at the discovery that it was itself and not something that the scholar would have liked better. . . "

This is, in fact, one of the repeated strengths of Bilbo as a character, and of the Hobbit race in general. They are themselves. Bilbo is just as he is, despite whatever the reader or the dwarves would do to improve him. Gandalf insists from the first that "Mr. Baggins has more about him than you guess," and this depth of character, imagination, and resourcefulness can only be recognized over a period of time. It is very much at the core of his method that Tolkien has his dwarves apply their assumptions and expectations about a "hero" to Bilbo, and find him wanting. The reader is inclined to do the same thing. Tolkien walks a thin line between the trivial and the extraordinary. Time and time again, through the small person of Bilbo, the accidental discovery of the tiny gold ring (just the size to fit a hobbit finger), and even the apparent slightness of this "children's story," Tolkien makes the point that even the smallest person or circumstance may have enormous impact and consequences. The surprising climax at the start of *The Hobbit* is surprisingly understated: "Suddenly his hand met what felt like a tiny ring of cold metal lying on the floor of the tunnel. It was a turning point in his career, but he did not know it." Taking an approach utilized by both Morris and the heroic poets, Tolkien reveals his messages through repeated motifs and patterns, rather than through the development of personality. The smallness of Bilbo in particular, and of the Hobbits in general and this children's story in particular, gains significance as part of a larger pattern of correspondences and conflicts between microcosm and macrocosm.

The pattern of narrative in *The Hobbit* could be seen as a spiral, widening in implication and connotation as the book progresses. The circle is further enlarged in *The Lord of the Rings*. Each of the smaller circles is, in turn, contained within the greater compass of *The Silmarillion*, the source and repository of all these tales. In this final book the rings are suddenly turned inside out, for it is both the beginning and the end of all the tales.

After Bilbo's adventure with the trolls, he makes the first of his tiny discoveries: "a largish key, though no doubt William (the troll) had thought it very small and secret." This key unlocks the trolls' cave and there they find two swords, and a knife just the right size for Bilbo to use as a sword. These blades, destined to play a larger part in the tale, are written upon with strange "runes" and the deciphering and translation of these unfamiliar words becomes a future task. In fact, emerging from this stone-age scene, we are here first introduced to the problem of translation or deciphering secret language which becomes another recurring theme. The scene with the trolls provides a curious contrast and parallel to the opening of the book. Bilbo had entertained his visitors to tea in a much more civilized version of the dinner party the trolls are having. Tolkien makes a point of observing the unmannered behavior of the trolls ("He took a big bite off a sheep's leg he was toasting, and wiped his lips on his sleeve. Yes, I am afraid trolls do behave like that. . . ") which is in some ways similar to the uncivilized intrusion of Gandalf and the dwarfs; matters are going from bad to worse as the layers of civilization are peeled away. The almost comical interruption of Bilbo's settled and well-mannered existence pales beside the close call with death at the hands of these trolls.

13

The third chapter, "A Short Rest," puts a cap on these first two adventures, and prepares us for a third descent which is to follow. We have spent the first portion of this journey descending and emerging from holes—the hobbit hole and the troll cave—and the seasons have shifted from spring to midsummer. It is on mid-summer eve, in fact, that a short rest produces its most interesting revelation. Studying the runes upon the swordblades, Elrond discovers that they are "very old swords of the High Elves of the West, my kin." He deciphers the names of the two swords: Orcrist, the Goblincleaver, Thorin's weapon; and Glamdring, Foe-hammer, Gandalf's blade. Finally the elf looks at Thorin's map and discovers moon-letters, runes which can only be seen in moonlight, containing a riddle-like instruction about the dwarf-cave's secret entrance.

Rest and reading play a significant and periodic role in the quest, but such interludes are always followed in Tolkien's stories by intense periods of action. The next chapter climaxes the series of encounters with holes, caves, and the unexpected. In fact, Tolkien tells us that Gandalf "knew that something unexpected might happen." The turn of events is signaled by a tremendous thunderstorm, "more than a thunderstorm, a thunder-battle." It is a foreshadowing of the vast forces which gradually come into play, for these are storms from the East and West making war: "The lightning splinters on the peaks, and rocks shiver, and great crashes split the air and go rolling and tumbling into every cave and hollow; and the darkness is filled with overwhelming noise and sudden light." Here is the meeting of high and low, of cave and lightning, of East and West. Symbolically it is a confrontation of the two extremes of light and darkness, dawn and sunset, the basis for conflicts throughout the great cycle of stories. The storm drives the party to seek shelter in a cave, and there they are attacked by goblins. Dori, carrying Bilbo on his shoulders, is jumped from behind, the hobbit rolls off into darkness, cracks his head on hard rock, and when he finally comes to, in the chapter entitled "Riddles in the Dark," he is in complete blackness.

The Hobbit is a children's story; the narrative technique, point of view, and comic or ironic tone which adds a lightness to even the darkest moments reinforce its appeal to a young audience. It nonetheless slowly builds and develops the characters, forces, energies and symbols which find their full maturity in the two works for adults. The encounter with Gollum is Bilbo's most famous adventure, and the cyclical images of the book are called to mind as Tolkien speaks of it as "a turning point." Bilbo finds the tiny ring, draws his small sword, and by its pale glow he begins to move forward to meet "Deep down here by the dark water"—"Old Gollum, a small slimy creature. . . as dark as darkness except for two big round eyes in his thin face." This descent is deeper and more alienated than anything in Bilbo's previous experience, and though all the details of it are small, it amounts to something of tremendous consequence. "At the very roots of the mountain," in the riddling game which follows, Tolkien echoes an archetypal schema. The scene recalls Odysseus in the cave of the cyclops Polyphemus, and Oedipus with the Sphinx. But Bilbo systematically exhausts the precedents of these earlier heroes. He is clever in his first simple riddles, but does not have the cleverness of Odysseus or the ingenuity of Oedipus. "Bilbo was saved by pure luck," Tolkien tells us; Bilbo yells out "Time," to beg for more time to think, and it turns out to be the correct answer to Gollum's riddle. Finally, the same type of accident causes Bilbo to mutter to himself, "What have I got in my pocket," and this becomes his insolvable riddle to Gollum.

It isn't entirely accurate to say that Bilbo's "pure luck" is absent from the earlier myths. There the "luck" is called fate, and it is ultimately the vast influence of fate which controls the events in this story. There is, however, another important mythic precedent which influences both our idea of fate, and our grasp of runes and riddles. Like Morris, Tolkien was an ardent admirer of Norse myth and legend. From that tradition Tolkien incorporates certain aspects of the conviction that the forces of good are fighting a losing battle against the forces of evil. In the Northern tales even the gods know there will come a day when they will be destroyed, and the burden is especially heavy for the sky-god Odin. He is preoccupied with the problem, and is unable to feast and celebrate with the other gods. He passes his food to two wolves which crouch at his feet, and learns from two ravens which perch on his shoulders—Hugin (thought) and Munin (Memory). Odin won knowledge of runes through suffering, and in doing so became a type of Christ figure—he did in fact hang on a tree, wounded with a spear, in order to master the magical power of Runes, characters which could be inscribed on metal, stone, or wood, and which had power to control the direction of events. Tolkien appears to affirm a more Christian version of the story, but he builds the suffering of his heroes gradually, making clear eventually that they must learn to bear the burden of being essentially alone, no more than pawns in an apparently losing battle with immense forces which will eventually crush them. During his alienated encounter with Gollum, Bilbo begins to assume the burden of powerful knowledge, a load which will be even more painful to his successor Frodo. Possessed of the ring, Bilbo becomes increasingly able to control and interpret events, and it is eventually he who properly interprets the runes. Even more directly parallel to the Odin stories, after Bilbo's accidental victory at riddles, he is attacked by wolves, and later saved by ravens.

"Riddles in the Dark" concludes the first five chapters, and forms a neat and symmetrical unity. This group of chapters is set primarily within the earth, in holes and caves, and the primary element is stone. The next section of five chapters begins with "Out of the Frying-Pan into the Fire," and follows the characters into the woods. There they encounter their enemies on top of the earth. First they are attacked by wolves, but are saved by Gandalf's setting fire to the forest, and are carried away from the flames by eagles, surviving a purification by fire. Journeying further into the wood, they are entrapped by spiders, and finally imprisoned in cave dungeons. They escape by water, floating to freedom inside empty wine barrels which take them to the Long Lake near the end of their Eastward journey; and there, for the first time, at the end of the tenth chapter and in the center of the book, the hobbits meet men.

By the mid-point in the story, Bilbo has been "there and back again" many times. Each episode partakes of the same structure as he moves into increasingly unfamiliar territory. The dark wood is a far less sympathetic environment than caves and tunnels which still have some resemblance to his own home.

And, in fact, imprisoned in the caves of the spiders, Bilbo begins to feel trapped like Sisyphus by cycles of repetition: "I am like a burglar that can't get away, but must go on miserably burgling the same house day after day." The Ring which can make him invisible has also isolated him from all the others, yet at the same time has made him responsible for saving them. He has survived trials of earth, air, and fire, and now escapes by water. Tolkien consciously plays upon the reader's assumption that there will be a happy ending. "But of course, as you have guessed," he writes, "he did rescue his friends in the end." In fact, we find that "only the river offered any longer a safe way from the skirts of Mirkwood in the North to the mountain shadowed plains beyond. . . .So you see Bilbo had come in the end by the only road that was any good."

The second half of the book repeats, in shortened form, most of the motifs and devices of the first section, again in symmetrical fashion. Though there is an exact symmetry in number of chapters—nine before the meeting with men, and nine after—the second half is far shorter, occupying only about half the number of pages as the first. This is in itself a comment that it takes longer to get "there" than "back again." The critic Randel Helms is unnecessarily puzzled when he complains about a "lack of structural coherence," and places the climax of the book in the finding of the Ring in Gollum's cave, and in the finding and *renouncing* of the Arkenstone in Smaug's cave at the end. This line of thinking leads him to discover his "symmetry of renunciation," which is certainly a key aspect of the book; in the very symmetry he mentions lies the story's structural coherence. It is far more appropriate to see both events in the words Tolkien himself uses when he describes the finding of the Ring. Both episodes are *turning points*, or in more symmetrical fashion, turn and return. The book's design is circular like the hobbit's door. It is most properly viewed as a single pattern, one completed circle, rather than conforming to the more traditional arrangement of narrative or thematic action rising to a climax. The total number of chapters in the story is 21—as in the tarot, where the total number of cards in the major arcana is also 21, the 21st card being a summary of all the preceding ones. The number itself—21— is said to express the reduction of a conflict ("2") to its solution or identity ("1"). The 21st chapter in Tolkien's book, "The Last Stage," perfectly completes the circle.

Within the full figure of a circle, Tolkien constructs a hierarchical reality, and its center is the central chapter of the book when we meet men for the first time. It is structurally correct that men, thematically the center, should also be physically centered in the chapters. The society of men is hierarchically ruled by a "Master." Thorin (whose name is a strong reminder of Norse mythology— Thor is the god of thunder) seeks to reinstate an old order, but the Master is given over to new and all-too-human concerns. The materialism of the Master is like that of the trolls, or as Tolkien says, of the goblins: "They make no beautiful things, but they make many clever ones." While songs at the beginning of the book had served to lure Bilbo away on this adventure, songs do not offer the Master himself a clue to the return of the King under the Mountain: "Nor did he think much of old songs, giving his mind to trade and tolls, to cargoes and gold, to which habit he owed his position." Here, despite position, "the matter was settled without him." The hierarchy is upset, and the old songs are revived in snatches as "others took up the song and it rolled loud and high over the lake." News of Thorin's return spreads "like fire through all the town," a remark which echoes the earlier encounter with fire and foreshadows the final fire from the dragon's throat which destroys and purges (purifies) the town.

The climax of the book, if we have to pick one, is the meeting with Smaug, the dragon, the great event to which all the adventures have been leading. The imagery of this final encounter presents the elemental symbols of the book in a unique and ironic series of reversals. Bilbo, the smallest and least significant in size, and initially the most reluctant to embark on the adventure, assumes ever-increasing importance in the events, greater degrees of intelligence and courage, and a mounting sense of isolation. At the very time that Thorin is about to regain his kingly position, he is made to look petty and ordinary; in fact, as we have discovered, the dwarves are not the most heroic sorts. Tolkien points out near the end that they are "decent enough people. . . if you don't expect too much."

As Bilbo descends this time, he goes toward a red glow, the slumbering fire of the sleeping dragon, and also encounters water in the form of rising steam. Smaug is a vast creature with wings—at once a worm and a bat. Bilbo's ears begin to throb with a surrounding sound: "This grew to the unmistakeable gurgling noise of some vast animal snoring in its sleep down there in the red glow. . . . " Here Tolkien pauses to point out a climax—or perhaps merely to indicate another turning point: "It was at this point that Bilbo stopped. Going on from there was the bravest thing he ever did. The tremendous things that happened afterwards were as nothing compared to it. He fought the real battle in the tunnel alone, before he ever saw the vast danger that lay in wait." The narrator claims to have trouble finding words: "There are no words left to express his staggerment, since Men changed the language that they learned of elves in the days when all the world was wonderful." But Bilbo has no trouble at all; bantering with Smaug is a breeze compared to his encounter with Gollum: "No dragon can resist the fascination of riddling talk and of wasting time trying to understand it. There was a lot here which Smaug did not understand at all (though I expect you do, since you know all about Bilbo's adventures)." Bilbo discovers Smaug's weak spot, and picks up the Arkenstone, fulfilling his role of thief or burglar. In being the very thing he has been asked to be, Bilbo incurs the speechless rage of Thorin. In fact, as both the narrator and Thorin find themselves speechless, it is fortunate that the hobbit has now become quite talkative and decisive. When Bilbo stands up and admits he has taken the stone, Thorin throws a fit: " 'You! You!' cried Thorin, *turning* upon him and grasping him with both hands. 'You miserable hobbit! You undersized—burglar!' He shouted at a loss for words, and he shook poor Bilbo like a rabbit!" At the time of Bilbo's most heroic action, the symmetrical renunciation of the Arkenstone which parallels the finding of the Ring, hobbit and rabbit are connected in a particularly belittling way. It is yet another case of reversed appearances and expectations, for Bilbo has actually gained in strength and moral stature in his handling of the Arkenstone, his willingness to give it away to prevent war. Significantly, he offers it to Bard the Bowman, the man from Dale who actually killed Smaug. The passing of the Arkenstone to Bard prefigures the passing of the torch to Men, who will come to their full inheritance in the new Fourth Age. Bilbo's renunciation is a gesture toward the future, unlike Thorin's puerile and possessive quest to recapture the past.

Amidst diplomatic confusion, the Dale is attacked by Orcs; the threat from outside prompts the quarreling factions to look to the present and unite. Bilbo is quickly knocked out of the action: "He put on his ring early in the business, and vanished from sight." Despite his invisibility, he is hit by a hurled stone and loses consciousness just after seeing Eagles flying to join the defense. More important than the actual battle to Bilbo is his return to consciousness: "When Bilbo came to himself, he was literally himself." He has achieved a spirit capable of renunciation, but he also has assumed custody of the Ring: though something of a hero, he is now very much alone.

When he regains consciousness and realizes the ring is still on his finger, Bilbo removes it and becomes visible once more. He returns to the world to find Thorin about to depart. On his deathbed, the old king takes back his harsh words and bids Bilbo, "Farewell, good thief." The treasure is divided and the hobbit returns home, full circle.

The Hobbit concludes with Bilbo's arrival in Hobbiton in time to retrieve the household furniture and belongings which are being auctioned off because he is "Presumed Dead." As his "last stage" he begins to celebrate the deeds in song; the chapter contains a reprise of Tolkien's gentle lyric, "Roads go ever ever on," and in fact Bilbo himself now "took to writing poetry." He also writes his memoirs, the story of which we have just read. In a spirit of subcreation, Bilbo concludes the work by contributing to the cycle of literature as he recognizes himself part of "the prophecies of the old songs" which "have turned out to be true."

III. THE LORD OF THE RINGS

The first edition of *The Hobbit* was published September 21, 1937, and sold out by Christmas. The English publisher Stanley Unwin asked Tolkien for more about the hobbits, happy to have a hit on his hands, but Tolkien had no more such stories to submit. He did send along several children's tales, including "Farmer Giles of Ham" and "The Lost Road," but these were not found to be suitable as sequels. What Tolkien wanted to publish was his "Lost Tales," *The Silmarillion*, but the sprawling, complicated, and disorganized manuscript was not only unlike *The Hobbit*, it was unlike anything being published for children *or* adults. After having one of his readers examine parts of it, Unwin wrote back to Tolkien that "it is a mine to be explored in writing further books like *The Hobbit* rather than a book in itself." Tolkien accepted this as a matter of course, and in his reply to Unwin agreed to give "thought and attention" to a sequel, although he would still hold on to his hope of publishing *The Silmarillion* one day. The 1937 letter, which Carpenter quotes in his biography, expresses the centrality of *The Silmarillion* to all Tolkien's writing: "I am sure you will sympathize when I say that the construction of elaborate and consistent mythology (and two languages) rather occupies the mind, and the Silmarils are in my heart. So that goodness knows what will happen. Mr. Baggins began as a comic tale among conventional and inconsistent Grimm's fairy-tale dwarves, and got drawn into the edge of it—so that even Sauron the terrible peeped over the edge. And what more can hobbits do? They can be comic, but their comedy is suburban unless it is set against things more elemental.''

The Hobbit may begin and end with suburban comedy, but with Sauron peeping over the edge, the book consistently suggests a serious side: alienation or isolation, greed, power, and powerlessness before unfathomable hierarchies of elemental and earthly forces. His second book, *The Lord of the Rings*, treats all these themes more profoundly and completely. For the next twelve years, Tolkien worked on an incredible, ever-growing manuscript, finally completing it in 1949. In his Forward to the first volume of a novel so long it had to be broken into three parts (six books), Tolkien tells us, "By 1918 all but one of my close friends were dead." The loneliness, isolation, and loss he treats were continuing personal elements which Tolkien was able to transmute in his "elaborate and consistent mythology." In the writing of his masterpiece, including the period during the second World War, Tolkien witnessed new deprivation and waste; against this background it is no wonder that his tale presents myth dominated by war and isolation.

The Fellowship of the Ring

The *magnum opus* begins with *The Fellowship of the Ring*, and the apparent emphasis on companionship is complex and ironic. Circumstances force individuals to unite or form alliances during the tale, but they are largely artificial rather than natural or instinctive alliances. they inevitably show strain at the edges, and finally collapse into a view of imperfect human nature whose triumph comes through luck or grace.

The unexpected party at the beginning of *The Hobbit* is playfully parallelled by a long awaited party to celebrate Bilbo's birthday at the start of *The Fellowship*, and anyone familiar with the long-delayed writing of the sequel will fully appreciate the irony of Tolkien's "long-awaited" opening chapter. We further appreciate the ironical fact that a party, usually a gathering for fellowship, is used in Bilbo's plan as a way to escape from all his friends and relatives, to set off finally and completely alone. Bilbo has lived a solitary existence insofar as we know from *The Hobbit*—no wife or family, only annoying and distant relations—but at the start of this new story we find that old Bilbo has developed a close rapport with his orphaned nephew Frodo, who has come to live with him. We seldom see the closeness of the relationship, however, for the two are immediately separated. In fact, it seems that part of their sympathy may be based on their recognition of one another as loners. Gandalf, too, is something of a lone ranger (as is Strider, the ranger they meet later), a nearly-perfect mentor to Bilbo in *The Hobbit*; he personifies independent and constructive use of alienated sensibilities. Gandalf's mission at the party is to oversee a smooth separation of Bilbo from his nephew and the rather oppressive relatives, and to supervise the more difficult sundering of Bilbo from the Ring.

Gandalf reaches successfully out of his solitary perspective because he constantly holds in view a broader understanding of general moral and natural welfare. His constructive missions in *The Fellowship* are first shown through his research into hobbit history: "Among the Wise I am the only one that goes in for hobbit-lore: an obscure branch of knowledge, but full of surprises." His scholarly researches and observations include a thorough investigation of the Ring itself. His findings convince him it is time for Bilbo to relinquish the treasure, and he shares some of his discoveries with Frodo as he urges the younger hobbit to take up the quest. Through his study of history, his knowledge of hobbits, and his ability to translate the mysterious runes inscribed upon the ring, Gandalf transcends his solitary experience, comprehending a wider sphere in order that his actions may be directed toward wisdom and goodness. He shares his learning with others and is a model for both Bilbo and Frodo, both of whom later become scholars and chroniclers themselves. Not only does dedicated study (especially of history and linguistics) enable one to overcome isolation, it also cultivates a depth of knowledge which is prerequisite to making choices in genuine freedom. ("Ye shall know the truth, and the truth shall make you free." John VIII:32)

Free will is of paramount importance in Tolkien's moral scheme, and in order to choose whether to use or destroy the Ring, one must know its origins and history. The Rings were forged by the Elven-smiths of Eregion, descendents of Feanor, who made the Silmarils in the Elder Days. Sauron pretended to help the Elves in this project, actually seeking to extend his own power for evil through their skill. Together they made the Seven Dwarf-rings and the Nine Rings of Mortal Men 'doomed to die,' and the lesser Rings of Power. Sauron's part in their creation bent the good intentions of the Elves, and Sauron made them all subject to control by the One Ring which he planned to forge with his newly learned Elven secrets. Fortunately, Celebrimbor, chief of the Elven-smiths, made three special rings of his own, which Sauron never touched. Known as the Three Rings of the Elven-kings, these were more powerful than the rest, enabling the Elves to heal, create, and preserve, and they functioned for good purpose until about ten years later, when, in Mordor's Chambers of Fire, Sauron forged his controlling Ring, the One Ring which is the focus of *Lord*. Celebrimbor instantly was aware of what had happened and hid the Three, but the Seven and the Nine, which had already been given to Dwarves and Men, fell under Sauron's spell. He was able to rule the bearers of the Nine completely, but Dwarves, who were always strong in resistance, were more difficult to master. Sauron lost the One at the end of the second age [the full tale is told in *The Silmarillion*] when Isildur cut the Ruling Ring from the hand of Sauron. This lifted the restriction on the Three Rings, which could be brought out of hiding and used once again. However, the One Ring turns up again in *The Hobbit*, and if Sauron can regain it, all the good works accomplished by the Three will be lost, and the minds of those who bear the other rings laid open to Sauron.

Gandalf explains the outlines of the situation to Frodo, and expresses his own conviction that an even greater power is determining the course of events: ". . . there was something else at work, beyond any design of the Ring-maker. I can put it no plainer than by saying that Bilbo was *meant* to find the Ring, and *not* by its maker. In which case you also were *meant* to have it. And that may be an encouraging thought.'' Despite encouragement from Gandalf, Frodo must freely make his own decision to bear the Ring, and he decides responsibly to try to end the threat of the Ring by destroying it in the Cracks of Doom. Even with his decision made, Frodo begins his quest with considerable confusion: ''For where am I to go? And by what shall I steer? What is to be my quest? Bilbo went to find a treasure, there and back again; but I go to lose one, and not return, as far as I can see.'' In seeking to destroy the Ring, this tiny Hobbit seeks to invoke an apocalypse. The breaking of this Ruling Ring will destroy the power of all the others; it will, in short, end a cycle and alter history forever.

The Hobbit was concerned with the origins of things from the individual hobbit point of view, and its primary setting was beneath the surface of the earth. If the controlling symbol of that novel is the cave, suggesting the womb and psychological subconsciousness, the setting of *The Fellowship* is the surface rather than the depth of the earth, suggesting the separation between appearance and reality and the need to bring some perception of depth to this surface. (History and scholarship, for instance, are ways of adding depth to superficial appearances.) *The Fellowship* is thematically concerned with appearances (and disappearances), and its opening scenes are primarily set in familiar geographies and recognizable inns or pubs. Frodo begins by manipulating appearances to suggest that he is moving to a less expensive house in an area where he had lived earlier, and he leaves with old friends rather than unfamiliar strangers like those who lured Bilbo away on his strange quest. The looming threat of the shadowy riders adds an ominous quality to the opening episodes, but during the first book (twelve chapters) of *The Fellowship* there is far less entrapment or containment than in *The Hobbit*. It is more or less a continuous superficial movement that takes Frodo, Sam Gamgee, Merry, and Pippin away from Hobbiton, to the house of Tom Bombadil, to the inn at Bree where they meet Strider, and finally to the edge of a river they must ford.

One of the interesting and symbolic events of this first book occurs when they have crossed the land of Farmer Maggot on their way to Frodo's new home. The farmer protects him, and escorts the travellers to join Merry, when: ''Suddenly he produced a large basket from under the seat. 'I was nearly forgetting,' he said. 'Mrs. Maggot put this up for Mr. Baggins, with her compliments.' '' There are not many couples (or women of any kind) in Tolkien's long story, and this gift from a united pair is a good omen for the trip. It is also a very positive symbolic action that Maggot, traditional image of death and decay, sustains, protects, and nourishes Frodo. His final appearance is connected with the central ring motif of the novel: ''They watched the pale rings of light round his lanterns as they dwindled into the foggy night. Suddenly Frodo laughed: from the covered basket he held, the scent of mushrooms was rising.'' The rings of light and their gradual disappearance suggest the triumph of Frodo's quest; the gift of mushrooms (a food which grows in dark and decaying matter) prefigures a death/rebirth motif that begins to develop in the book. The mushrooms make a wonderful feast in a warm kitchen to celebrate the first successful portion of their journey, and the pleasure of it is doubled since Tolkien tells us: ''Hobbits have a passion for mushrooms, suspassing even the greediest likings of Big People.''

From the beginning, Frodo is fairly certain of his direction and generally in control of things as he moves over the surface of the earth. He understands his mission, even though there are haunting uncertainties and hidden dangers ahead. The episode with the farmer he had known as a child points up Frodo's adulthood. Frodo is far more adult from the outset of his quest than Bilbo was; he has joined a great contest in which every adult must consciously choose a side. Whereas Bilbo was tricked into his adventure, Frodo sets forth as a free agent fully understanding the significance of his choices.

The day after their meeting with Farmer Maggot, the hobbits enter the old forest, and Frodo's companions are trapped inside a willow tree—an action strongly parallel to the sanctuary they had found inside a hollow tree at the start of their trip. They are saved when Tom Bombadil comes along, singing a song which opens the tree. The hobbits are introduced to the compelling power of music over nature—of art restoring harmony to the natural world; human joy and goodness used in a positive way to counter the forces of confinement. Tom Bombadil is exuberant, radiant, vital, and, like the farmer, married. As they approach his home, his merry song is echoed by his wife's: "Then another clear voice, as young and as ancient as Spring, like the song of a glad water flowing down into the night from a bright morning in the hills, came falling like silver to meet them." It is the most beautiful sentence in the book thus far, and "with that song the hobbits stood upon the threshold, and a golden light was all about them." Tom is a master of natural forces, "of wood, water, and hill." His mate is Goldberry, "daughter of the River." Though Tom never explains exactly who he is, he is addressed as "Master" in an almost religious sense. His own answer to the question of his mastery is strikingly parallel to God's response to Job: "Eldest, that's what I am. Mark my words, my friends: Tom was here before the river and the trees; Tom remembers the first raindrop and the first acorn. . . He knew the dark under the stars when it was fearless— before the Dark Lord came from Outside."

Whatever force or power Tom represents, it is clearly an ancient power of light, and a power greater than any mere tokens or trinkets. He asks Frodo to see the Ring, and Frodo, "to his own astonishment," unchains it and hands it over. "It seemed to grow larger as it lay for a moment on his big brown-skinned hand. Then suddenly he put it to his eye and laughed. For a second the hobbits had a vision, both comical and alarming, of his bright blue eyes gleaming through a circle of gold. Then Tom put the Ring around the end of his little finger and held it up to the candlelight. For a moment the hobbits noticed nothing strange about this. Then they gasped. There was no sign of Tom disappearing! Tom laughed again, and then he spun the Ring in the air—and it vanished with a flash. Frodo gave a cry—and Tom leaned forward and handed it back to him with a smile." Here is another foreshadowing; it may eventually be possible for the ring, rather than the bearer, to disappear.

In pointing out that Tom's is a world of "mortal neutrality," Randel Helms only scratches the surface of an enigmatic and powerful force. Tom has always been close to hobbits, and they have told many tales about him; it may be that this close bond is one reason why the hobbit is an appropriate creature to bear the Ring. Despite his "moral neutrality," Tom seems to be on the side of light and of goodness, and he once again rescues the travellers when they are captured by Barrow-wights. The connection between Frodo and Bombadil is further strengthened by the fact that Frodo's travelling name, Mr. Underhill, links him directly to Tom who has his home "down under Hill" and who sings of his lady waiting there. In fact, in teaching Frodo to sing his song, there is the suggestion that Tom willingly shares his power in some sense.

The vigor and laughter of Tom Bombadil lifts the story's pace and tone considerably. The episode also significantly expands the surface aspect of the journey in directions of depth, height, and time. Tom's scope extends deep "under Hill" into the earth, but he seems equally in control of the element above the earth with his trick of tossing the Ring into the air where it disappears. His temporal history reaches back before the beginning of time, and forward to predict that "the Sun would shine tomorrow," and that their "setting out would be hopeful," and the hint that the Ring just might eventually disappear. Superficial catagories of time and space melt with respect to Tom; under his influence they see "in their minds pools and waters wider than any they had known, and looking into them they saw the sky below them and the stars like jewels in the depths," and "Whether the morning and evening of one day or of many days had passed Frodo could not tell."

With Tom's help the travellers take up their path again and escape the living-dead clutches of the Barrow-wights. They press on to the "Sign of the Prancing Pony," an inn at Bree. There Frodo appears to try to imitate Tom's disappearing act. Caught up in a party spirit when the guests call for a song, Frodo sings a long and "ridiculous song that Bilbo had been rather fond of" about a beer-drinking Man in the Moon; as he sings he capers "about on the table; and when he came a second time to *the cow jumped over the Moon*, he leaped in the air. Much too vigorously; for he came down, bang, into a tray full of mugs, and slipped, and rolled off the table. . . He simply vanished, as if he had gone slap through the floor without leaving a hole!" He had given in to a strong impulse to put on the ring, and thereby had reenacted a scene similar to Bilbo's in the first chapter when he vanished before his party guests. It is an unfortunate indulgence which nearly tips their enemies to the fact that they have the Ring, but through this indiscretion they fortuitously come to know Strider—later called Aragorn—who has skill enough to guide them along their way.

With Frodo's disappearance the first full circle of the book has been completed and a new cycle begins. They set out secretly, this time led by Strider, who, like Gandalf, "was learned in old lore, as well as in the ways of the wild." As in their first expedition, they are fearful of dark riders. They approach the tower of Weathertop where there is a "wide ring of ancient stone-work" and there detect, they think, a message scratched by Gandalf, but the visit also gives away their position, for they are clearly visible silhouetted at the summit. Strider explains that their dark pursuers "do not see the world of light as we do but our shapes cast shadows in their minds, which only the noon sun destroys; and in the dark they perceive many signs and forms that are hidden from us: then they are most to be feared." Strider helps them comprehend the different modes of perception of these dark forces, and Frodo understands how lucky he is to have gotten off at the Inn with his lame excuse about crawling away under tables. The dark vigilance perceives in a different mode. This recognition is followed quickly by a direct encounter. They are surrounded by "three or four tall black figures. . . . So black were they that they seemed like black holes in the deep shade behind them," and Frodo hears "a faint hiss as of venomous breath." Frightened and overcome by an impulse to put the ring on, Frodo yields and instantly sees the figures clearly, five of them: "In their white faces burned keen and merciless eyes." But as soon as Frodo wears the ring, he is visible to his enemy as well, and as they stab him he feels a "pain like a dart of poisoned ice pierce his left shoulder."

In the following chapter, "Flight to the Ford," he is carried along by his companions, overcome by a deep and consuming cold. Though they reach the Ford with the help of Glorfindel, Book I ends as "Frodo felt himself falling, and the roaring and confusion seemed to rise and engulf him together with his enemies. He heard and saw no more." Because in a sense Frodo dies here, later to be reborn, this is the first of the death-rebirth cycles which ripple outward from the Farmer Maggot episode. It is part of Frodo's education, a hard and painful lesson, but finally hopeful because of his recovery; and the death-rebirth motif reflects Tolkien's Christian understanding of how one recovers from loss to be reborn through a process he describes in his essay "On Fairy Stories" as "Recovery, Escape, Consolation."

At the end of the first of the six books which comprise Tolkien's novel we can already begin to appreciate the monumental quality of the work. Increasingly the prose reads like words chiseled on stone. Word choice is striking and purposeful, precise and immutable. If for no other reason, Tolkien must be respected and remembered for having built this beautifully crafted monument. The towering size of the novel is entirely appropriate to the scope and compass of the struggle it depicts. It is nearly the opposite of a conventional novel, which more usually portrays the struggle within a single soul; Tolkien's struggle is of a cosmic order, a conflict of elements about to rip apart, as when two weather fronts meet and a vast storm results: ice and fire; thunder and lightning. Tolkien's moral tempest is not given to excess, however. The form of the work is firm, strong, and concise. Despite its length, this is a lean book—partly a result of the deliberate process by which it was written, for it was built slowly, as an ancient Ent would build, with no thought of responding to cries that it must be done quickly. Tolkien accomplishes something new in fiction partly because this fantasy was no mere passing fancy, but carefully written and framed strictly according to the author's principles. As Tolkien told Stanley Unwin, "It is written in my life-blood, such that it is, thick or thin; and I can no other."

The structure of Tolkien's fiction shows a distinction born of slow time, the twelve years he spent writing and revising it. He once said of it, "I don't suppose there are many sentences that have not been niggled over." This results in richness, not only of surface action, but of underlying unified literary structure which makes criticism of it challenging and rewarding. There are always repeated discoveries in re-readings. One can read Tolkien, like Shakespeare, many times with pleasure.

The novel has been skillfully divided into "Parts," and further rendered into "Books" and "chapters" which function like the movements of a symphony. The orchestrations and tempos shift, but the movements never repeat unnecessarily; what's more, they never lose the integrity which comes of a comfortable wedding of form and subject. The form does not suffer from the imposition of ulterior motives—no suspenseful endings solely to bring the readers back for the next periodic installment, no structures dictated merely by the limitations of a stage, a printed form, or any particular conventions. There is a great integrity about Tolkien. One sees immediately that his writing is not done for economic success or even for scholarly acclaim. The enormous popularity of the results of this steady craftsmanship proved to be as surprising to him as it was to his publishers.

Tolkien's steadiness and patience in assembling his fiction convey his ability to operate effectively within time; his fiction itself reveals a preoccupation with temporal reality. Book II starts in October, one year from the time of the story's beginning. Thus far events have followed a chronological order with only hints of timelessness, as in the Tom Bombadil episode. But time is about to be more dramatically interrupted. At the opening of Book II we journey into the realm of the Elves where time has no significance in our familiar terms. Thereafter, the book begins to deviate from strict chronology, using flashbacks and replays of simultaneous events seen from various perspectives. One by one Tolkien is shedding the contrivances which tie his reality to ours; his tale concerns a timeless conflict. In fact, as we move into the novel we are asked continually to enlarge our conception of time. The widening of the temporal limits closely parallels the ripples of significance radiating from the tiny hobbit outward to the limits of the moral universe.

The opening of the second book recalls us to the small center of it all—the fragile existence of this single hobbit Frodo: "Frodo woke and found himself lying in bed." We are back in the realm of purely subjective time where the book began, "When Mr. Bilbo Baggins of Bag End announced that he would shortly be celebrating his eleventy-first birthday." A string of temporal locations place Frodo immediately in a different context: "At *first* he thought that he had slept *late*, after a *long* unpleasant dream that still hovered on the *edge of memory*." In the course of that single sentence we sweep from present time into a more abstract historical past. His first words are, "Where am I, and what is the time?" He receives a definite response: " 'In the house of Elrond ["Elrond" = "the round"—the ring or circle motif again?], and it is ten o'clock in the morning,' said a voice. 'It is the morning of October the twenty-fourth, if you want to know.' " Gandalf explains that Frodo is safe among the Elves and has been cured by Elrond; after "three days, to be exact" he has arisen from his illness. Dead and reborn, it is as though Frodo begins his entire quest anew on another level. Tested and strengthened, he has completed a cyclical progression, rising in a gyre.

Time and destiny are increasingly conspicuous in this chapter. Since time in the land of the Elves passes differently, the pace of movement is considerably altered from the first book, where time was constantly crucial—from Bilbo's carefully-timed birthday disappearance to Frodo's ill-timed wearing of /
to the neck-and-neck race at the Ford. In Rivendale Frodo learns he m

on his own, not supported by the mission of Bilbo, or the urging of Gandalf, or even the assistance of Maggot or Strider. Gandalf tells him simply, smiling: "You are the Ring-bearer. And you are the heir of Bilbo, the Ring-finder." As he enters Elrond's gardens, Pippin cries out in courtly fashion: "Here is our noble cousin! Make way for Frodo, Lord of the Rings!" Gandalf quickly corrects the mistake: "Evil things do not come into this valley; but all the same we should not name them. The Lord of the Ring is not Frodo but the master of the Dark Tower of Mordor, whose power is again stretching out over the world! We are sitting in a fortress. Outside it is getting dark."

In Rivendell Frodo discovers another reality far beyond him in age, stature, and scope. Elrond, son of Earendil the Mariner, bears the Great Ring Vilya, strongest of the Three. Seated at his table, Frodo feels "very small," especially as he is overwhelmed by the beauty of Elrond's daughter Arwen. Frodo also finds that Bilbo has taken up residence there, and his stature as historian and artist has significantly increased. As Bilbo sings the beautiful story of Earendil (a name for Venus in the Cynewulf Crist), he is depicted "in a circle of listeners," a confirmation that the power of the Ring in Bilbo's case has been transformed into art. Bilbo has become a subcreator; he celebrates images in what Tolkien calls in his essay "a higher form of Art, indeed the most nearly pure form." That Bilbo should be so honored by Elves, who themselves create the most beautiful songs and lovely language, is a high honor indeed. Frodo can see in Bilbo a former Ring-bearer who has been artistically elevated by the experience. Frodo's grasp of his own identity as bearer enlarges as he contemplates the ancient achievements of the Elves, and the more recent accomplishments of his kinsman within this sphere of timelessness.

Gloin the Dwarf also helps enlarge the perspective as he speaks of events in *The Hobbit* and explains that there is in dwarves, as in all the peoples of the world, a sense of grave loss at the passing of old time: "We make good armour and keen swords, but we cannot again make mail or blade to match those that were made before the dragon came." Here, as in the case of Tom Bombadil, ancient existence is shown to be superior. Tolkien's treatment of history is built from his own Catholic religious background, with the Fall (and Satan) clearly dividing the primal golden age from the present, fallen history. Frodo's symbolic death and resurrection after three days may suggest he is a savior. He has sacrificed himself, has *chosen* the path of sacrifice, and as a result of this he awakens in this "timeless" Ring world of Rivendell. Yet the real question in *Lord of the Rings* is not redemption to a heavenly state, but survival with the acknowledgement of loss, and continuing existence in a post-lapse reality which has as its final promise not victory, but endurance. Frodo's mission within time is to sacrifice the Ring. Temporarily removed from time, he can more clearly see past glory and the fall. Yet though that past can never be recovered, through great faith and suffering the fallen present can work to limit the power of evil, the cause of increasing deterioration, and the force which must be prevented from complete triumph at all costs.

Tolkien completely eschews the idea of progress. The purpose of human action is not to build an improved City of God, but merely to prevent the fragments and ruins of the old city from disappearing completely. Bilbo never understood any of this, though as historian and artist he does help to preserve the golden past through stories and songs which hold the feelings and spirit of those magnificent old times. Frodo as a member of the younger generation is called upon to live more fully in the present, and to accept the physical, as well as the spiritual and artistic sacrifices which the call to high moral purpose necessitates.

Together with the sense of a lost grandeur in the past and a preoccupation with its preservation, there is also in this chapter a look toward the future. Most obviously, the convening of the council to determine the outlines of their mission is one forward look toward survival and sacrifice. But in a fleeting glimpse, Frodo intuits (and Tolkien foreshadows) the end of it all as he gazes at the Elves: "Elrond was in his chair and the fire was on his face like summer-light upon the trees. Near him sat the Lady Arwen. To his surprise Frodo saw that Aragorn stood beside her; his dark cloak was thrown back, and he seemed to be clad in elven-mail, and a star shone on his breast." Arwen is said to have been the exact likeness of Luthien, "the Evenstar of her people," a compliment to Venus Earendil whose story Bilbo sang, an image reflected in the star on Aragorn's armor, and, finally, an image of completion of yet another ring or cycle. We may well ask ourselves whether the Evenstar appears at the beginning or end of a cycle. We should remember that Aragorn is the last Heir of Isildur, descendent of Elendil, who had uttered the prophecy: "Out of the Great Sea to Middle-earth I am come. In this place will I abide, and my heirs, unto the ending of the world."

In the Council of Elrond, the story of the Ring is told completely for the first time: "A part of his tale [Elrond's] was known to some there, but the full tale to none, and many eyes were turned to Elrond in fear and wonder as he told of the Elven-smiths of Eregion and their friendship with Moria, and their eagerness for knowledge, by which Sauron ensnared them. For in that time he was not yet evil to behold, and they received in aid and grew mighty in craft, whereas he learned all their secrets, and betrayed them, and forged secretly in the Mountain of Fire the One Ring to be their master." If knowledge brought about their downfall, however, perhaps a different kind of knowledge may lead to salvation. All the characters are strengthened in knowledge by both enquiry and events, but of all the central figures, Gandalf seems most directly in touch with special knowledge. His scholarly ability to decipher old texts is similar to Tolkien's, and proves frequently significant in plunging beyond the surfaces of objects or actions: "There lie in his hoards many records that few can now read, even of the lore-masters," Gandalf explains concerning Elrond's library, "for their scripts and tongues have become dark to later men." The House of Rivendale is a place of learning; it reflects Tolkien's professional life devoted to illuminating ancient texts to students at Oxford. (With the publication in trade editions of his translations of *Sir Gawain*, *The Pearl*, and *Sir Orfeo*, they can be enjoyed by a wide reading public as well. These texts were in great danger of dropping altogether from general knowledge, and Tolkien is to be greatly praised for bringing them to our attention again.) By associating Gandalf and others with high scholarly pursuits and linguistic skills, Tolkien makes it clear that knowledge *per se* is not the reason for the fall. The pursuit and preservation of knowledge can be a route to great strength (as with Gandalf); it can be allied, in

27

fact, to what Tolkien calls "subcreation."

The problem the council faces is a technological one. How can they keep the Ring safe forever? They consider handing it over to Tom Bombadil, but Glorfindel believes "in the end, if all else is conquered, Bombadil will fall, Last as he was First; and then Night will come." The Ring is oddly like nuclear waste. The problem is how to keep it safe *forever*—and the answer is simply that there is no way to guarantee this. The alternative is to abandon the power of the Ring entirely; to destroy it. As Sam sensibly observes as the end of the council, "A nice pickle we have landed ourselves in, Mr. Frodo!"

The Council agrees on a company (or fellowship) of nine, "and the Nine Walkers shall be set against the Nine Riders that are evil." Those who go on the mission elect to do so of completely free will, and "no oath or bond is laid on you to go further than you *will*. For you do not yet know the strength of your hearts, and you cannot foresee what each may meet upon the road." Tolkien does not tell his company what path to choose, but he does point out the need to make a choice. A basic tenet of Tolkien's moral system is his affirmation of free choice. The choice itself predetermines the end, for the spirit of the choice, and one's remaining true to that choice, seem more important than any specific events or actions. Tolkien hammers home the point in both explicit discussions among characters, and in actions and directions of the narrative. In the second part, Gandalf will call Sauron out from his tower, and ask even this deadly enemy to make his choice once more. In true Christian spirit, Tolkien seems to say through Gandalf that even this black villain, deeply ensnared in evil, could choose once more finally for good and be forgiven.

The iteration of the choice motif stresses that life is continuous choosing, that for Tolkien, every minute of time must represent a choice, and if the choice is made in a spirit of generosity, integrity, and courage, it will not threaten a good final result. This is an assertion which is existential and apocalyptic simultaneously. It affirms the importance of the present moment in which the action of free will defines identity, and it holds out the possibility of sudden reversal of that identity by a future choice. Perhaps appearances do not reflect the real state of affairs because they are often not in accord with Will; Sauron ensnared the Elven-smiths because "he was not yet evil to behold." There is always the chance that choice will be made on the basis of false appearances, so one seeks the basis for decisions elsewhere, beyond the superficial realities of time and appearance.

Tolkien develops the idea that the Will is potentially the most powerful force in the tale, and that it can see beyond the surfaces. Strength of will compensates for the insignificant stature of the heroic hobbits, whose appearance belies their actual strength. Will is not a physical matter, though it affects physical matter; strength of will is not particularly affected by size. (This point is made perhaps most dramatically in Sam's encounter with Shelob in *The Two Towers*.) One expression of the idea is found in a remark Bilbo makes to Frodo as they speak together for the last time before the quest. Echoing Gandalf's supporting comment about Bilbo in *The Hobbit*, he says, ". . .just a plain hobbit you look. . . .But there is more about you now than appears on the surface." Bilbo has outfitted Frodo with the Elven mail and presented him with the short-sword Sting (a marvelous name, comical almost, and seemingly insignificant, like the hobbits). Henceforth we progress below the surface in action and morality; always returning to the level pattern of their journey, the company descends and ascends to perspectives which enable different points of view.

As the company sets out toward Moria they begin a descent in both space and time. They move toward the great pit, and toward the past (and future). Moria may be linked to *moira*, the Greek word for fate, for the entire tale of Moria has about it the sense of irresistible destiny. In fact, theologically, the Elvish name meaning "given without love" suggests a somber pagan backdrop where fate is unredeemed by Will (redemption is always linked to love in Tolkien's writing—consider, for instance, the love between Sam and Frodo; or Beren and Luthien). Deep beneath the surface of the earth, they discover the fate of Balin and his crew, and, threatened themselves, they escape across the Bridge of Khazad-dum (the last syllable echoes "doom"). Gandalf is locked in struggle with Balrog, and falls with the monster into the pit. The Fellowship is broken: "They looked back. Dark yawned the archway of the Gates under the mountain-shadow. Faint and far beneath the earth the slow drum-beats: *doom*. A thin black smoke trailed out. Nothing else was to be seen; the dale all around was empty. *Doom*. Grief at last wholly overcame them, and they wept long: some standing and silent, some cast upon the ground. *Doom, doom*. The drum-beats faded."

The remaining party continues into Lothlorien, there to gain a new perspective on *doom*, and to see, in the Mirror of Galadriel, a future in the surface of the mirror, as well as to glimpse a past far deeper than anything they had imagined. Within Lothlorien Frodo "found his hearing and other senses sharpened," and "it seemed to him that he had stepped over a bridge of time into a corner of the Elder Days, and was now walking in a world that was no more." Lothlorien (Loath to lose lore?) is the most dramatic presentation of reality beyond the surface thus far. This land is a breakthrough in Tolkien's scheme, and through it several patterns become clear: surface time is isolated by the discovery of the radiating depth of time as it gathers meaning in the past and future. Yet simultaneously (and not without irony) the surface definition of fellowship is also destroyed, as tenure in Lothlorien results in the disintegration of the original, obvious, and external form of the band of nine. In Haldir's remarks only a few sentences later, however, he forecasts an optimistic end to "estrangement," with significant implications for the development of a new sense of fellowship: "The world is indeed full of peril, and in that there are many dark places; but still there is much that is fair, and though in all lands love is now mingled with grief, it grows perhaps the greater."

At the center of all the virtuous forces of light and of goodness, Tolkien shows us love. His presentation of this central human ideal is unique and intriguing, for he has presented it as an *idea* and a *feeling* lacking any hint of sexual passion. Love in Tolkien assumes an ideal medieval quality—a beatific *caritas*. His book is practically unique in twentieth century literature in its strange depiction of this central value, increasing in significance during the course of the great work. It is not accidental that the notion of "love" begins to gather meaning at the very time the external fellowship is forced to dissolve.

The highlight of the visit to Lothlorien is a meeting with the Lady of Galadrim (glad dream?), and their look into the Mirror of Galadriel (glad, real?), Sam, who eventually expresses love more openly than any other character in the tale, offers a prelude to the mirror by observing that he feels "as if I was inside a song, if you take my meaning." The statement reminds us that we are inside a novel, inside a song—box within box. We ritualistically approach an inner ring described in various images: "the circle of white trees," a treeless space "running in a great circle," "a green wall encircling a green hill." As we approach the inner sanctum, Haldir explains, "In this high place you may see the two powers that are opposed one to another: and ever they strive now in thought, but whereas the light perceives the very heart of darkness, its own secret has not been discovered. Not Yet." We observe from a high vantage point, while Tolkien's reminder that we are inside rings of fiction, song, and nature gives us a feeling of probing far below the surface. We remain technically on the surface, but *Fellowship* is deeply concerned with non-material, aesthetic, and moral choices. Here we become explicitly aware of the absolute opposition of two material powers—thesis and antithesis, light and dark—the outer limits of choice.

The Lady of Galadrim is the great White Goddess toward whom the narrative has slowly moved. She represents not so much an apotheosis of love as an inspiration to choice. Free will becomes a refrain in her advice; the company must choose constantly and truthfully: "I will not give you counsel, saying do this, or do that. For not in doing or contriving, nor in choosing between this course and another, can I avail; but only in knowing what was and is, and in part also what shall be." Choice, the Lady suggests, can be moved beyond the surface by the dimensions of time. The lesson of scholarship and learning, the knowledge of past and speculations concerning the future, these may be called upon to inform and support choice. Like the Greed gods, subject themselves to fate, even the Lady is not exempt from the necessity to choose. Frodo offers her the Ring, and she contemplates herself as a terrible goddess, "dreadful as the Storm and the Lightning!" She seems transfigured even as she speaks: "She stood before Frodo seeming now tall beyond measurement, and beautiful beyond enduring, terrible and worshipful." But she laughs and breaks the spell. "I will diminish," she says quietly, "and go into the West, and remain Galadriel." Having met her test, she knows simply, "now we have chosen, and the tides of fate are flowing."

The company leaves Lothlorien together, but the seeds of separation are growing; each member's choice and path must be his own. The last glimpse of Galadriel is especially appropriate to this, as it shows her in lovely isolation: "Alone and silent. As they passed her they turned and their eyes watched her slowly floating away from them. For so it seemed to them: Lorien was slipping backward, like a bright ship masted with enchanted trees, sailing on to forgotten shores, while they sat helpless upon the margin of the grey and leafless world." One of the extraordinarily lovely passages in Tolkien, and noteworthy for its magical simile, this foreshadows the end of *The Lord*. As the mystical other-worldly present distances itself from them, they are surfacing again, returning to the plain and ordinary world, the world that goes on.

Frodo, nearly misled by Boromir, realizes he must continue his mission alone—except for Sam who, aided by his close knowledge of his master, concludes just in time that Frodo would have gone for the boats: "Back to the boats! Back to the boats, Sam, like lightning!" As Frodo and Sam set off on the last stage of the quest together, they are linked by the image of lightning— a flash of sudden insight through empathy—by their past companionship, and by a bond of love and dedication, man to man, which makes clear a fellowship far deeper than any we have yet seen.

The Two Towers

With the introduction of the diametrically opposed forces at the end of *The Fellowship*, Tolkien paves the way for spiritual conflict and spiritual growth beyond the superficial level. The second Book in *The Lord* takes its title from a material structure. If the basis of the first book was "fellowship"—a movement depicting the *joining* of individuals and peoples and races for a great purpose, followed by an apparent sundering of the peoples into individual or fragmentary units at the end—this second book is concerned with structures rising above the common level in life, and rising in both spiritual and material planes toward confusion. The tower is traditionally symbolic of ascent and is often emblematic of pride, as in the Tower of Babel. In traditions stemming from both Egyptian and Medieval sources (and preserved, for instance, in the tarot), the tower is the primary structural form stressing verticality, with windows at the topmost level; it corresponds to man, with eyes and mind at the top. Seen under this aspect, the Tower of Babel represents communal disorder and blasphemous ambition; the tower in Tolkien's novel, with its searching eye, is a similar symbol. In the tarot, by the way, the tower's most disturbing image of disaster is shown in the sixteenth card of the major arcana, an image of a tower struck by lightning.

In the forceful image of the tower in Frodo's early dream, and in its recurrence at the end of Book II, Tolkien foreshadows and develops the tower symbol. The conclusion of *Fellowship* enlarges the metaphor. Boromir, possessed by the dream of power, throws Frodo into a state of confusion. Frodo puts on the Ring and disappears. Then, "leaping blindly" (a blind leap of faith), he climbs to the top of Amon Hen. There within a "wide flat circle" is a high stone chair: "He was sitting upon the Seat of Seeing, on Amon Hen, the Hill of the Eye of the Men of Numenor." ("Noumenon" is a "thing in itself," as distinguished from a phenomenon, or thing as it appears, Kantian rather than Hegelian philosophy.) The Seat of Seeing is a place of exercise for the eye and mind, a tower image, allowing him a vision of the two towers facing one another, white against black, across an abyss of space and a chaos of conflict: "All the power of the Dark Lord was in motion. Then turning south again he beheld Minas Tirith. Far away it seemed, and beautiful: white-walled, many towered, proud and fair upon its mount-seat; its battlements glittered with steel, and its turrets were bright with many banners. Hope leaped in his heart. But against Minas Tirith was set another fortress, greater and more strong. Thither, eastward, un*will*ing [note *will*] his eye was drawn. . . wall upon wall, battlement upon battlement, black, immeasurably strong, mountain of iron, gate of steel, tower of adamant, he saw it: Barad-dur, Fortress of Sauron. All hope left him. And suddenly he felt the Eye. There was an eye in the Dark Tower that did not sleep." In *Fellowship*, then, Frodo has moved from his tiny hobbit hole to the great hill of vision. *Towers* begins upon the towering hilltop of Amon Hen, where Aragorn this time takes the stone seat and looks out. Guide and mentor until now, Aragorn suddenly sees far less than Frodo: "The sun seemed darkened, and the world dim and remote. He turned from the North back again to North, and saw nothing save the distant hills, unless it were that far away he could see again a great bird like an eagle high in the air, descending slowly in wide circles down toward the earth." Both Frodo and Gandalf have moved beyond the surface dimension, and even the consistent flow of time begins to be interrupted. From Aragorn's limited perspective on the summit, he cannot grasp the importance of the bird descending from the air in its wide rings of flight, but soon Gandalf will explain that this is how he returned. Though his vision is dim, Aragorn hears the sound of Boromir's great war horn and runs quickly to try and help.

The two towers clearly are emblems for two points of view; and as they stand dialectically and diametrically opposed, they represent the thesis and antithesis of fellowship, as well as of other moral characteristics. The initial external fellowship is broken, but each member of the party will fulfill a purpose toward one final vision. Randel Helms observes in *Tolkien's World* that "the actions of the sundered group are as necessary to the overall quest as Frodo's journey itself." The two major victories of Book III—when Sarumen is defeated at Isengard and the Orcs are overwhelmed at Helms Deep—must take place before Rohan's ride to Gondor.

Though he doesn't see great revelations from this hill of vision, Aragorn nonetheless reaches a significant new understanding, a gift of insight more than foresight: "My heart speaks clearly at last: the fate of the Bearer is in my hands no longer." There is a controlling force which shapes events beyond any single character in the drama; Aragorn bows to this power. It is as though he attains an unspoken understanding of the need for each will to make its own choice, and for each character to play an individual role. Aragorn, Legolas, and Gimli—man, elf, and dwarf—set out to find the Orcs who have captured the two hobbits, Meriadoc and Peregrin. Though the hobbits are still paired at the start of the book with an apparent fellowship, by the end of Book Four, Merry and Pippin have been separated, and even Samwise and Frodo have been isolated from one another. This isolating process occurs at the very time we become aware of a great meshing of events which may eventually create a larger fellowship of spiritual purpose, unified through action for common intent to coalesce in a final victory; at least this is what the reader hopes. Despite the appearances of greater force by the dark powers, the two victories presage triumph for a less outwardly apparent type of strength.

Another aspect of Tolkien's message in the separate adventures experienced by members of the fellowship has to do with the nature of the spiritual battle. Collective action and unified attack don't seem to be appropriate metaphors for the spiritual strength Tolkien advocates. Time and time again the spiritual decisions of the most consequence are faced by individuals alone. The common good will of each action taken separately links the small and isolated pieces into a purposive movement, but neither the characters nor the readers can fully recognize the larger conjunction of events until after the fact. These aspects are presented stylistically and structurally as well as thematically; Tolkien begins to deviate from straight chronological narrative, repeating adventures and stories from various individual perspectives until we ourselves are led to see how they coalesce. At the same time the style becomes more formal and elevated, it also becomes more psychologically close and colloquial as it reflects first-person thoughts of various characters.

At the opening of Book III Aragorn seems to understand how he may be contributing to the larger purpose: "Ours is but a small matter in the great deeds of this time." He follows the task at hand, content that the small part be played well, that *someone* should try to help Merry and Pippin. The Orcs who captured them have gotten hopelessly far ahead. They try to read the story of the hobbits' fate from tracks and trails and faint footprints and they are on the right path even though they are somewhat misled by the appearance of the tracks. At last they recognize, exhausted, that "they were alone in a grey formless world without mark or measure." The fellowship finds itself dislocated and dispersed.

At this low point of isolation and dislocation, the company meets with the Riders of Rohan, and events are somewhat illuminated by their news. Tolkien continues to make us aware that we are at once in the midst of a story and a cycle of legend and heroic myth which, like the tales being recorded by Bilbo, will eventually shape the book we are reading. Up to this point the characters have essentially *received* tales, backgrounds, and information. We can recall the strenuous research performed by Gandalf before he confronted Bilbo and Frodo with the full weight of the Ring—and the increasing bits of knowledge, history, and magical-mythological lore which were slowly bestowed upon the characters in *Fellowship*. Henceforth it seems to become the function of the isolated characters to *tell* tales rather than receive them, and it is in the attempt to explain the origins and backgrounds of hobbits that one of the Riders exclaims, "But they are only a little people in old songs and children's tales out of the North. Do we walk in legends or on the green earth in daylight?" "A man may do both," says Aragorn. "For not we but those who come after will make the legends of our time." Aragorn's reply illustrates the new internal perspective he has attained; from the brief and dark outlook of the hill of vision until the end of Tolkien's narrative, Aragorn is shown building upon and slowly dispensing his store of increasing inner-directed wisdom.

Herein lies another strength of Tolkien's tale, and one of its special areas of appeal to the American sensibility. He reminds us of the process through which we integrate imaginative self-consciousness with a larger enduring world of art and society; individual experience is preserved in myth and legend. For the American reader especially, this notion seems to be something many of the "founding fathers" and pioneers were aware of. More than any other modern nation, the American people have been conscious of building and living in the shadow of their own myths and legends. This has been especially true of the American relation to the land, of frontier America, expressed, for instance, in Turner's "frontier thesis," and echoed by Aragorn: "The green earth, say you?

That is a mighty matter of legend, though you tread it under the light of day."

Aragorn by implication says that we inhabit two dimensions: the world of actual events, and the legends about those events which will follow. The goal should be to sense both the surface and the depth, the immanent and transcendent event, the passing time on this green earth celebrated timelessly in legend and in song. Awareness of both will clarify rather than confuse, particularly as it applies to the question Eomer raises about how a man can make sound judgments in chaotic times: "Good and ill have not changed since yesteryear; nor are they one thing among Elves and Dwarves and another among Men. It is a man's part to discern them as much in the Golden Wood as in his own house." Moral truth is one thing: continuous and unchanging. It contains the dichotomies "good" and "evil," which apply universally to all types of life in Tolkien's fiction—to all the varied creation of the world. A man's good judgment for Tolkien, as for the founding fathers, is based on self-evident truths.

The meeting of hobbits and Ents illustrates the timeless aspect of these truths, and a convergence of apparently opposed or opposite appearances. It is a meeting of large and small, and continues the spatial emphasis on verticality suggested by the towers of the title. The tree-like Ents are clearly allied to "the green earth," organic rather than technological (like towers), and their ancient sense of judgment between good and evil is not deceived by technology nor the insignificant size of the hobbits.

Chapter II, "The Uruk-Hai," leads up to the hobbit-Ent encounter through chronological flashback. It is the beginning of winter, symbolically the dead season, a dormant period which nonetheless serves as prelude to renewal and rebirth. At a time when the "fellowship" is physically alienated and divided, Tolkien's writing style takes us intimately into the minds and thoughts of individual characters. Pippin awakens with a headache, disoriented and confused; as he reconstructs events for himself, they become clear for the first time to the reader. Pippin and Merry, belying their names, are miserable, haunted by "evil dreams and evil waking. . . blended into a long tunnel of misery, with hope growing ever fainter behind." The Orcs who convey the hobbits down this tunnel can run untiring for miles, as if they are engines of some terrible technology. They are clearly beasts, primitive and animalistic on the one hand, with their "filthy jowl and hairy ear," but they are slaves and mechanical servants because they have relinquished their individual identities to the power and command of the Dark Power which first created them. In this they are linked to abstract technology, power unredeemed by human consciousness, "unresting, as if they were made of wire and horn, beating out the nightmare seconds of an endless time." Time has practically no meaning to these slaves, because their lives have essentially no meaning. Even the language they speak seems indecent, like "a foul taste: 'Ugluk,' 'Grishnakh,' Lugdush.' " Tolkien is a superb inventor of words, the best in English since Jonathan Swift.

When the contemptible Orcs are encircled by Riders, Merry and Pippin are able to slip away unseen and enter the ancient woods. As when they first were sheltered in *Fellowship* within the hollow trunk of a tree, the forest offers sanctuary to the hobbits, and Tolkien tells us that this ancient setting may serve as a path for renewal when he describes the hobbits: "little furtive figures that in the dim light looked like elf-children in the deeps of time peering out of the Wild Wood in wonder at their first Dawn.''

The contrast between Orc and Ent is extraordinarily clear and direct. They are opposites in nearly every way, though the length of their names suggests a parallel. The Orcs are superficially speedy, can run tirelessly forever; the Ents are superficially slow and awkward, but their movements are full of considered intention and therefore consequence and endurance. The Orcs are killed off practically by the dozen and they seem to be totally expendable in time, while the Ents are as long-lived as they are tall. Pippin's description of the impression Treebeard's eyes made on him shows the depth: "One felt as if there was an enormous well behind them, filled up with ages of memory and long, slow, steady thinking: but their surface was sparkling with the present: like sun shimmering on the outer leaves of a vast tree, or on the ripples of a very deep lake. . . . it felt as if something that grew in the ground—asleep, you might say, or just feeling itself as something between root-tip and leaf-tip, between deep earth and sky—had suddenly waked up, and was considering you with the same slow care that it had given its own inside affairs for endless years.''

The open, full language of the Ents is in marked contrast to the heavily consonanted and strident language of the Orcs. Treebeard's favorite expression, "Hrum, Hoom" has the full and humming sound of a religious "OM." His playfulness with language is reminiscent of Tom Bombadil: "Hoom, hm; hoom, hm, how did it go? Room tum, room tum, roomty toom tum." Unlike Tom, however, Treebeard's wordplays have more self-consciousness behind them, less of the free exuberance and near-nonsense playfulness: "There are Ents and Ents, you know; or there are Ents and things that look like Ents, but ain't, as you might say." This rich linguistic awareness becomes explicit as Merry and Pippin explain the shortened forms of their names, and Treebeard replies, "my name is growing all the time. . . so my name is like a story. Real names will tell you the story of the things they belong to in my language, in the Old Entish as you might say."

Treebeard explains that the Ents are "tree-herds," and in this they are like shepherds, traditional Christian figures, except that they tend more ancient flocks. They are representative of a druidical or primeval consciousness, repository of unconscious history in an archetypal Jungian sense. The forest was historically among the first places in nature to be dedicated to the cult of the gods, and the tree has been symbolically viewed as an axis linking different worlds which correspond to its roots, trunk, and branches. It figures forth the continuity of the cosmos and inexhaustibility of the life process. In decorative Eastern art the central tree is called *hom* (another echo of the "om" and "hoom"), the cosmic tree. But in many traditions there are two trees—"Tree of Life" and the "Tree of Death"—or "tree of the knowledge of good and evil" and the tree (cross) Christ hung upon to redeem the sins of the first tree. In Tolkien's mythology, as we fully learn in *The Silmarillion*, the Two Trees are originally both trees of light, but in the fallen world there is a conflict between tree and tower; it was Sauron's master Morgoth who poisoned the two trees and created the chain of events which left Sauron ruler of the Dark Tower. If we metaphorically extend "Two Towers" to include this contrast of tree and tower, we see clearly the dialectic of technology versus organic nature, division (head-quartered in the isolated technologically-constructed tower and personified in the mindless slave-fellowship of Orcs) versus unity (the genuine fellowship of choice and principle which is united even when its members are separated and scattered; the organic "tree-herding" mission of the Ents), and ultimately of evil versus good. Again, the greater strength is not where it may at first appear to be. The Ents seem clumsy, slow and old, but Treebeard explains, "We are made of the bones of the earth. We can split stone like the roots of trees, only quicker, far quicker, if our minds are roused! If we are not hewn down, or des-troyed by fire or blast or sorcery [technology], we could split Isengard into splin-ters and crack its walls into rubble."

Chapter Five constitutes another shift in perspective as we rejoin Man, Elf, and dwarf; and it introduces The White Rider, Gandalf, returned from the grave among the renewals of this wintry season. Merry and Pippin have begun their rebirth from Orc captivity, the Ents are roused from a trance-like hiber-nation to action, and Gandalf returns in a radiant new form, having been vic-torious over the powers of darkness. Here at the center of the three-part novel, Gandalf exclaims, "We meet again. At the turn of the tide. The great storm is coming, but the tide has turned." From here to the end of the book, Tolkien simultaneously develops cycles of rebirth and destruction, the working out of choices already made. The slow divided world of middle earth begins to join and to ally itself, no longer unaware and alienated. Sure knowledge of the outcome is yet in doubt, but Gandalf expresses a central philosophical statement, per-fectly in keeping with Tolkien's own brand of Christian faith: "Have patience. Go where you must go, and hope!"

Where they must go first is to the Golden Hall at Edoras where Gandalf seeks to renew the weak and aging King Theoden. He rids the king of his mis-leading counsellor Wormtongue, using a familiar symbol of power: "There was a flash as if lightning had cloven the roof. Then all was silent. Wormtongue sprawled on his face." Gandalf brings a simple message: "The storm comes, and now all friends should gather together, lest each singly be destroyed." His ability to wield lightning shows some control over the elements of storm, and embodies the quick jolt of apocalyptic judgment which can reverse the tide of deceitful words once emanating from Wormtongue. Henceforth, there is a gradual uncovering of deception, and a renewing of ancient or deluded persons, peoples, and powers. King Theoden can declare himself no longer "an old tree under winter snow" (a metaphor which links him to the Ents), observing that "a west wind has shaken the boughs" in such a way that new life, not death, has been the result.

Gandalf hurriedly departs on Shadowfax to carry out other business, and Gimli, Aragorn, and Legolas ride on with Theoden to the tower at Helm's Deep where the first large victory awaits them. There, at the head of Deeping Comb in the northern White Mountains, a complex of fortifications and towers guards the entrance to the gorge. Standing on the walls, Aragorn and the others watch the vast Orc armies mount their attack. Lightning, which in the early parts of the tale was often used as an expression of surprise or unexpected insight, now becomes part of the storm of war, the fearful clash of opposites, where the "arrows thick as the rain came whistling over the battlements," and "lightning tore aside the darkness." As the men of the Mark gaze out from the battlements, "It seemed to them. . . a great field of dark corn, tossed by a tempest of war, and every ear glinted with barbed light." The natural, organic fertility image of corn and the striking power of "barbed light" convey the essence of this struggle involving physical power (manifest in lightning, technology, the tower of stone, magic, the Ring, the flashes from Gandalf's staff) and natural growth (increments of growth in human nature, the gardening of Sam Gamgee, the trees, the organic forcefulness of the Ent). The dark Orc forces have cut down the trees and converted them to mechanical weapons: "In their midst they bore two trunks of mighty trees. . . . The trees, swung by strong arms, smote the timbers with a rending boom." Though the barriers seem horribly vulnerable to this incessant pounding, even as the last barricades begin to crumble, Gandalf, the White Rider, returns with the Ents in full force: "The land had changed. Where before the green dale had lain, its grassy slopes lapping the ever-mounting hills, there now a forest loomed. Great trees bare and silent, stood rank on rank." The clear victory of these living forces over dead technology is assured: "The Orcs reeled and screamed and cast aside both sword and spear. Like a black smoke driven by a mounting wind they fled. Wailing they passed under the waiting shadow of the trees; and from that shadow none ever came again."

Tolkien depicts case after case of power pitted against power. The state of the universe is shown to be constant struggle, a contest of wills. The forces of magical or contrived power, shaped by a fervent will for power over others, are not to be dismissed or underestimated—but the ancient organic forces carry the day. Tolkien affirms the goodness and strength of the original creation, and his loving affirmation of nature is odd, in a way. As a scholar, Tolkien spent much of his time inside the library or study—closed environments, rather like the cozy holes the hobbits love. Some of the most significant activities in the great struggle of *Lord* take place within tombs, rooms, and towers, rather than in the free and open gardens or forests of the natural world, so Tolkien doesn't neglect the scholarly environment he knew so well. He shows us a desirable alliance in which both natural impulse and intellect, the forest and library, have their equal share.

The allies led by Gandalf ride on to Isengard, where they find the great fortress laid waste by the Tree-folk; Saruman and Wormtongue are isolated in the Tower of Orthanc. This citadel of Saruman has "(by design or chance) a twofold meaning; for in the Elvish speech *orthanc* signifies Mount Fang, but in the language of the Mark of old, the Cunning Mind." Scholarship and linguistics never leave our awareness, and we might interestingly recall that the Ents were first contacted in the Forest of Fangorn, so this has been a clash of fang against fang. The Ent Treebeard is particularly aware of names and the meanings of words, and may be seen as an "organic scholar." His is the application of mind without cunning, the difference, perhaps, between the two sorts of "fang."

It is not merely the organic nature of the Ents which assures their power, but also their ancient roots. Of the various hierarchies in Tolkien's world, the hierarchy of age and history seems the surest. The oldest things are nearly always best, and in the final volume, when Gimli and Legolas reflect upon rebuilding the ruins, they explain this as a natural progression of events since the beginning. It is another metaphor, this time a seasonal one for the Fall: "And doubtless the good stone-work is the older and was wrought in the first building," Gimli says. "It is ever so with things that Men begin: there is a frost in Spring, or a blight in Summer, and they fail of their promise." The best thing about the ancients is that they established the promise, the potential, and that this established principle has itself endured. It is, therefore, a promise of hope for the future, as well as an expression of great potential from the past.

The overthrow of Sauron is like a literalization of the Birnham Wood episode in Shakespeare's *Macbeth*, and indeed the power of an Ent is frightening, not only because one does not *expect* this, but also because much of its force has to do with harnessing what are normally slow changes over long time: "An angry Ent is terrifying. Their fingers, and their toes, just freeze onto rock; and they tear it up like bread-crust. It was like watching the work of great tree-roots in a hundred years, all packed into a few moments."

Time assumes a different though related emphasis in the hasty and untimely anger of Wormtongue when he throws down the Palantir from the tower, in the anger of the moment tossing away one of Sauron's greatest treasures. The *palantir* were made for communication, but they soon became instruments for control rather than mere means for exchange. The globe of the palantir, like a television set, or telephone, enables the user to communicate across great distances instantaneously, defying space and time. Alone, each one "could do nothing but see small images of things far off and days remote," but linked together, they form another net of slavery. It very nearly proves the downfall of Pippin as he succumbs to the temptation of a thief, gazes into the stone, and is revealed to Sauron.

Book IV backtracks in time, even though Gimli has just complained in the last chapter of the previous book "We are beginning the story in the middle. I should like a tale in the right order. . . ." In fact, as we once again meet up with Sam and Frodo, they are in the process of "sometimes retracing their steps because they could find no way forward, sometimes discovering that they had wandered in a circle." It becomes a question whether Tolkien has adopted a circular or linear model for the temporal dimension of his book. Essentially, time seems cyclic, mistakes repeated, seasons turning, until the symbolic circle which encloses the entire book—the Ring—can be destroyed; if it can, then time can resume a progressive, forward motion. It serves as a principle of good literary form that the temporal organization of the story should reinforce or repeat this thematic point. Frodo senses the entrapment and frustration of cyclic time in his retraced steps, exclaiming, "I wish I could come there quickly and make an end!" But instead, Frodo is entangled in another circle as he once again meets Smeagol/Gollum, and very nearly tames him.

Frodo's forgiving treatment of Gollum is prompted by awareness of large temporal units, and his own sense of fulfilling a kind of circle begun by Bilbo. While he is considering what to do with the captive, Frodo "quite plainly" hears voices from the past, discussing Bilbo's treatment of the monster, and he recognizes the virtues of Pity and Mercy (Tolkien capitalizes them) in Bilbo's conduct. He forms his actions not merely based on the present-time situation, but responding to the dialogue of past voices: " 'Very well,' he answered aloud, lowering his sword. 'But I am afraid. And yet, as you see, I will not touch the creature. For now that I see him, I do pity him.' "

Tolkien reiterates that the events of the world take place instant to instant, apart from any predetermination from earlier times. Every instant of time is in some sense timeless, for the choices made at every moment have the potential for changing the course of all future time and the meaning of past time. Pity, Mercy, Forgiveness are the qualities which make it possible to assume this about time: those driven by greed, possessiveness, hatred are tied irrevocably to the past Fall and to time. Frodo's act of mercy seems to touch something deep in Gollum, to remind Gollum that he might not be as bad as he has been: "At once Gollum got up and began prancing about, like a whipped cur whose master has patted it. From that moment a change, which lasted for some time, came over him. He spoke with less hissing and whining, and he spoke to his companions direct, not to his precious self."

Randel Helms points out the numerous close parallels between books III and IV: "In each book of the second volume, a hobbit pair must traverse a seemingly impossible distance (III) or impassable area (IV) in a limited amount of time, and in each, they succeed only because of the reversed effects of evil intentions upon them (Saruman's, Gollum's). After the crossing, each hobbit pair encounters a figure of authority in a forbidden land (Treebeard in Fangorn, Faramir in Ithilien), who has been drawn there by rumor of enemy encroachment on his territory, and led to the specific location of the hobbits in each case by the sight of smoke (the Orc cremation, Sam's cook-fire). In each case, that leader must decide whether to kill or help the hobbits. He decides in both cases to help, but the decision to kill is narrowly averted by the wise and generous refusal to act hastily. . . .After parleying, the hobbits proceed with the authority figure to his cave, where they get their first good meal and safe rest in a long while. The hobbit pairs then proceed on their quests, each of which ends in the destruction of a dark tower (Orthanc, Barad-dur)."

Helms's study is excellent in making many of the parallels and patterns of this complex fiction clear, and although Daniel Grotta-Kurska calls his work a "bad book" in his bibliography, arguing that it "misses the point of the work entirely by attempting to apply Freudian analysis to the characters and themes," Helms's application of Freud is not nearly so inappropriate as this reaction might suggest. The parallelism noted by Helms gradually comes to undergird the fabric of Tolkien's universe, so that in the end, the parallels and correspondences are affirmed and endure, while the dichotomies and contradictions are negated and perish. It is extremely important to note these, for their presence illustrates a vision of the world based on support rather than force—and the parallel actions of the scattered members of the fellowship triumph precisely because they are aimed in common directions by independent wills, unlike the forces of Sauron, which can be bent only by the ruling Eye, all subject to the force of a single will.

It is sometimes said that John Milton wrote the only genuinely English epic, but the validity of the statement is modified by Tolkien's masterpiece. The epic proportions of this tale establish new standards for the form in English. Tolkien has elevated novelistic fiction through the epic traditions, and through the formal and poetic rhetoric of his style; and he has taken unique advantage of the intimacy of the novel format to add more personal perspectives to the epic range. In proper epic fashion, the tale unfolds *not* as an allegory (a tendency Milton could not avoid), but as a complex fictive work where *allegoresis* is extended within parallel structures to convey significance and theme, and to establish a clear moral direction without mere reduction to moralistic formulae.

In the place of "epic hero" Tolkien has given us a cast of heroic types, both nobler and less noble than we see in our ordinary selves. While some critics have taken him to task for one-dimensional characterization, Tolkien has chosen to play by different rules than those applying to characterization in normal fiction, giving us a range of heroic options rather than a single introspective hero. It must be said, however, that introspection is not absent from this book. *The Two Towers*, as it deviates from a straight chronological narrative, and follows the characters into isolated states, also increasingly shows us glimpses of their inner thoughts. Throughout the book these "good" characters are gaining strength and stature—Frodo and Gandalf most obviously, with Sam Gamgee next in importance, and Aragorn, Merry, and Pippin rising to increasing prominence (Merry and Pippin even literally gaining in size after they have sipped the Ents' draught).

Sam's importance is highlighted at the conclusion of *Towers*, after Gollum has led them by the only way they could have entered Sauron's empire, along the stairs of Cirith Ungol. As they near their destination, Gollum yields increasingly to his evil inclinations and his desire for the Ring, and Sam and Frodo find they are left entirely to their own resources. Sam is able to make some moderate sense of their situation on the basis of old tales, the ancient tradition of tale-telling which Tolkien constantly affirms and continues through both scholarship and "subcreation." Responding to Frodo's complaint, "I don't like anything here at all," Sam reasons, "We shouldn't be here at all, if we'd known more about it before we started. But I suppose it's often that way. The brave things in the old tales and songs. Mr. Frodo: adventures, as I used to call them. . . . Folk seem to have been just landed in them, usually—their paths were laid that way. . . . But I expect they had lots of chances, like us, of turning back, only they didn't. And if they had, we shouldn't know, because they'd have been forgotten. We hear about those as just went on—and not all to a good end, mind you; at least not to what folk inside a story and not outside it call a good end. . . I wonder what sort of a tale we've fallen into?" Tolkien provides the exchange as a bit of comic relief, but he also reminds us again, as he does at various crucial points in the story, that the telling and preserving of tales has a positive effect on character and on history. It makes us aware of another dimension, and can enable us to perceive our own circumstances under a different light. In this tense situation, Sam has lightened the atmosphere, and goes on to refer to a specific tale, Beren's fetching of the Silmaril, a "long tale" that "goes on past the happiness and into grief and beyond it." Then Sam realizes,

"Why, sir, I never thought of that before! We've got—you've got some of the light of it in that star-glass that the Lady gave you! Why, to think of it, we're in the same tale still! It's going on. Don't the great tales never end?"

With the reference to the Silmaril, Tolkien explicitly reminds us again of the interconnectedness of his subcreated world. (We can learn more of "the tale" in his posthumously published *Silmarillion*.) The connection is revealed in terms of *light*. For here in this black hole, Frodo and Sam meet the most evil woman of the tale, Shelob: "The most loathly shape that he had ever beheld, horrible beyond the horror of an evil dream. Most like a spider she was, but huger than the great hunting beasts, and more terrible than they because of the evil purpose in her remorseless eyes." In the face of this horror, the happy and unexpected recollection of the light they have brought with them (a gift from the *best* woman in the tale!) serves to assure their survival—and the light is part of an ancient tale which they themselves are part of. Into these eyes of evil purpose without remorse, Sam casts this light: "The beams of it entered into her wounded head and scored it with unbearable pain, and the dreadful infection of light spread from eye to eye. She fell back beating the air with her forelegs, her sight blasted by inner lightnings, her mind in agony." Lightning from a clear sky, as C. S. Lewis said? In a sense, it is, for Sam's clear, ordinary thinking has put him in touch with this light. From here to the end of *Lord*, "lightning" gathers significance for Sam and Frodo, for it is their small light shining in the darkness of Mordor which will provide the only hope for Middle Earth.

One final point needs to be stated here. Lightning in the book is to be expected from the black storm clouds Sauron gathers about his dark forces. It is quite another thing when that light streams from unexpected places to shatter the darkness: when it is wielded from the White Gandalf, or by the clear-sighted Sam. When it is elven light, Galadriel, it is glad.

The Return of the King

From the caves and surfaces of the earth to the towers of Part II, Part III constructs a synthesis which reviews all of these locations, returns us to our point of origin, and then takes us, with Bilbo and Frodo, toward a new element: onto the High Seas and into the West. The final episode is the most sweeping and grandiose, yet also includes the intimate union of Sam the gardener with his Rose at the end, and provides a hopeful and moving conclusion to the cycle.

Whatever new information we learn in the final volume of Tolkien's great work, the key word in the title is "Return." The extent to which the vision offers paradise regained may be debated, but there are significant returns for nearly every character, particularly celebrated in the ceremony of the return of the king which unites Gondor and Arnon, and which the title stresses. In the end, both the hobbits and the readers return to the place they and the tale began, to Bag End, where the narrative ends both for Sam and for us. We watch the ship bearing Elrond, Galadriel, Gandalf and Frodo sail off into a place we cannot see—whether that final destination will mark a return or a beginning is impossible to answer on the basis of the evidence presented in the final pages of the tale.

Perhaps the departure of these monumental characters is one signal of an element in the conclusion which is not suggestive of return: that key structuring principle of the entire work, time, does not return. Indeed, Tolkien clearly indicates the limits and boundaries of time as he repeats in various ways the motif, "The Third is over."

"The Return of the King" for Tolkien means the embodied restoration of ideals of virtue, harmony and justice. To be sure, the organization of Tolkien's society is hierarchical, but we should recognize that the *ends* are far more important than the *means*. The principle of free action reiterated throughout the tale in Tolkien's references to free choice and the significant role played by even the least of the hobbits and others stresses the individual importance of each action and the free decision-making which forms the crux of good fellowship. We may also see something in all of this of Tolkien's deep Catholic faith, for Catholicism more than any other Western religion has postulated an actual shape of hierarchical authority stemming from God who is represented by specially endowed earthly surrogates.

In marked contrast to the communist society in William Morris's fantasy, Tolkien's utopian conclusion presents a thoroughly unrevolutionary patriarchal monarchy. It is both English and Arthurian, but it is also thoroughly Catholic, a fact we can never forget in exploring Tolkien's subcreation. His new age can easily represent an England reborn in something of what the divinely ordained kingship once was supposed to mean. It is free, but undemocratic. The background of trivial characters, including many of the other Baggins clan (especially the Sackville-Bagginses!), clearly shows the proletariat in an unheroic, unintelligent, inconsequential light. Again, it contrasts markedly with the consistently 'noble' characters populating Morris's utopian fantasies. But Tolkien does not eschew or belittle the trivial—in fact, in the case of Frodo, he has elevated the lowly to a place of prime importance—for it is, even in this hierarchical society, the common people, the political proletariat, who must always act as Ringbearer.

The Return is concerned with the restoration of order, with a universal rebirth which has been prefigured in the progressive deaths and resurrections of many of the principle figures and climaxed in the apparent death/resurrection of Frodo at the end of *Towers*. It remains for the King himself to undergo the process, which we witness in the final volume, and for the whole social and natural order to follow then in this resurrection cycle. Tolkien makes it clear that resurrection is selective: we also witness irrevocable destruction in this final book. . . irreplaceable loss, a hard but ineluctable reality. We will witness triumph and defeat, the return of the king and the return of the hobbits, and finally, as readers, we face the end of the tale; we lose not only Bilbo, Frodo, and Gandalf as they disappear into a vast and faceless ocean, we also lose the entire secondary world of this great fiction.

Tolkien has shown us cave, surface and tower, and this final volume recapitulates the lot: the triumph of the White Tower and the descent to an ambiguous victory at the Cracks of Doom. The governing principle of this volume, however, is the fourth dimension of time. Temporal realities and confusions have grown more complex in the evolving scheme of the work as a whole, but they loom enormously in the conclusion which will demolish the very continuities of time in a transcendent apocalypse which ushers in a new Age. Even this temporal perspective is broadened and deepened with the appendices to the entire work, presenting "Annals of the Kings and Rulers," "The Tale of Years," "Family Trees," the "Shire Calendar," and a specific note on "Calendars" in general. Tolkien has made clear from the start that the destruction of the Ring will destroy *all* the existing rings of power, and will mean a loss of power for good as well as evil: our labor in the struggle will begin anew, according to different rules, and we see the start of it in the hobbit's more mundane struggle with Sauron, and the tenacious survival of Saruman and Wormtongue. It is interesting that we are more convinced of the loss of the good guys—Gandalf/Bilbo/Frodo—than of the bad, whom we suspect will probably not have put in their last appearance.

Part III begins simply: "Pippin looked out from the shelter of Gandalf's cloak." *Return* starts psychologically close to Pippin, and the tale will slowly depict heroic achievements by both Pippin and Merry—relatively untainted and genuinely heroic achievements, unlike the dubious triumph of Frodo. Frodo and Bilbo are corrupted by the mysterious powers of the Ring, and both of them perform the role of "thief" to the end.

Merry, Pippin, and Sam are relatively untouched by it and can move innocently and energetically into the New Age. The image of Pippin protected by Gandalf's cloak—an image which reflects his innocence—is in marked contrast to the stripped and beaten Frodo, who is painfully scarred by the harshness of his experience at the end of Tolkien's work (and these scars are linked to time, recurring most painfully like a stigmata on the anniversary of their reception). Pippin is caught up in a "swift-moving dream" and wonders if he was awake or still sleeping. He is out of touch with time ("Sleepily he tried to reckon the times and stages of their journey, but his memory was drowsy and uncertain") while Gandalf urgently and desperately maneuvers within it, shouting to Shadowfax, "We must hasten. Time is short."

They arrive at Minas Tirith and we catch our first glimpse of the White Tower. Minas Tirith is in fact another name for Minas Anor, "Tower of the [setting] Sun," set against Minas Ithil, "Tower of the Moon"; having been captured by the Nazgul, Minas Ithil began to be called Minas Morgul, the "Tower of Sorcery," and Minas Anor was then renamed Minas Tirith, "Tower of Guard." Minas Tirith is a great stone city built on seven levels. It is an image of endurance, but also exemplifies a decay from past grandeur. The features which Pippin observes even in his "growing wonder" are those of an abandoned ghost-town: "Yet it was in truth falling year by year into decay; and already it lacked half the men that could have dwelt at ease there. In every street they passed some great house or court over whose doors and arched gates were carved many fair letters of strange and ancient shapes: names, Pippin guessed, of great men and kindreds that had once dwelt there; and yet now they were silent, and no footstep ran on their wide pavements, nor voice was heard in their halls, nor any face looked out from door or empty window." The sense of loss, of unrecoverable vanished beauty, is one of the great themes of this final part, a growing sense of bittersweet pain at what has been lost (the memory of Numenor, the fairest City in the west of Middle Earth; the irremediable loss of the Ent-wives) and what will be lost with the ending of the Third Age. This haunting sense of loss is present to the leaders of this age, and is constantly figured forth in the eloquent dead tree at the center of the city—an image echoed again in the final pages of the book with the death of the Hobbiton party tree under which the whole story began.

The slow complication of narrative established during the first two parts of *The Lord* coalesce completely in the final volume. Beregond begins to explain to Pippin the scope and urgency of the mission Gandalf has been so long in arranging. "We are caught now in a great net and strategy," he tells Pippin, and the young hobbit comprehends the depth of the situation in the cry of a Fell Rider of the air: "It is the sign of our fall, and the shadow of doom." Beregond expresses another aspect of Tolkien's theme as he describes hope and memory as the two great consolations from our inevitable loss: "Though all things must come utterly to an end in time, Gondor shall not perish yet. . . . Hope and memory shall live still in some hidden valley where the grass is green."

The mature narrative power Tolkien demonstrates in *Lord* comes fully into view as we begin to recognize the chords of his great themes clearly, and to marvel at the "great net and strategy." Tolkien has been misjudged by some critics who have not clearly known or approved of the origins of his genre in the fiction of Morris and MacDonald, and in the epic and saga traditions. Morris in particular developed a fantasy form which depicted heroic life within time and history as a struggle for commonwealth (another way of saying fellowship). Critics attacking both Morris and Tolkien for broad and clumsy characterization, for instance, are misjudging their work. As Tolkien himself explained in his essay "On Fairy-Stories": "Drama is, even though it uses a similar material (words, verse, plot), an art fundamentally different from narrative art. Thus, if you prefer Drama to Literature (as many literary critics plainly do), or form your critical theories primarily from dramatic critics, or even from Drama, you are apt to misunderstand pure story-making, and to constrain it to the limitations of stageplays. You are, for instance, likely to prefer characters, even the basest and dullest, to things. Very little about trees as trees can be got into a play." Tolkien's narrative achieves "pure storymaking" of a kind and scope certainly beyond that of drama, and is able to render the importance of *things*—rings, trees, rocks, towers—in eloquent detail. "It was in fairy-stories that I first divined the potency of the words, and the wonder of the things, such as stone, and wood, and iron; tree and grass; house and fire; bread and wine," Tolkien says. Morris created these things anew in his fantasy worlds as Tolkien does in turn, rendering them in startling narrative clarity because in fantasy they are "freed from the drab blur of triteness or familiarity."

Tolkien simplifies the general purposes of his narrative art in characterizing the "functions" for fairy-stories: "Recovery, Escape, Consolation." Recovery, of course, presumes loss. In the case of the beloved "things," much of that loss was occurring in Tolkien's real world: the trees were being chopped down, the housing was being made ugly and impersonal, the war had changed the shape of

England and combined that loss with the deaths of many of Tolkien's closest friends, and the drastic modern assault on Oxford had begun. These things were among those which made the loss both personally tangible and humanly difficult for him. Tolkien himself understood all too clearly that "the way men were living and working in the twentieth century was increasing in barbarity at an alarming rate." In fact, the description of the blighted landscape near the end of *Two Towers* is not unlike what was going on in England as a result of rapid technological growth: "They had seen scars of the old wars, and the newer wounds . . . a pit of uncovered filth and refuse; trees hewn down wantonly and left to die. . . ."

Tolkien wrote of our twentieth-century plight as "self-made misery," and felt that the fantasy which might help us to escape from and improve this condition must not let us forget the moral corollary of this misery: "We are acutely conscious both of the ugliness of our works, and of their evil. So that to us evil and ugliness seem indissolubly allied. We find it difficult to conceive of evil and beauty together. . . . Even more alarming: goodness is itself bereft of its proper beauty." The only force which Tolkien can imagine capable of reversing the self-selected path of twentieth century barbarism must be apocalyptic in design. In "On Fairy-Stories" he speaks of it as "the good catastrophe" and gives it a special term, *Eucatastrophe*. This is the conclusion of the great war in *Lord*, a good catastrophe which brings certain loss, but which also cleanses and renews the possibility for beauty and moral direction in the age to come.

"On Fairy-Stories" is indispensable reading for anyone wishing to understand Tolkien's purpose in narrative; the painful sense of loss, and the memory and hope by which this loss is bearable, are found in his formula: "Recovery-Escape-Consolation." Fantasy is the best form of literature in which to present *Eucatastrophe* because it is, in Tolkien's terms, more purely "literature," has more narrative art and less dramatic art about it. Moreover, it is a place where genuinely "new form is made." These new forms are what Tolkien calls "subcreation," and they stem from his Christian belief that man is made in the image of a Creator: "We make in our measure and in our derivative mode, because we are made: and not only made, but made in the image and likeness of a maker." The details of the theory of "sub-creation" were explored by Tolkien in conversations with C. S. Lewis and other friends, and are summarized in Carpenter's biography: "We have come from God (continued Tolkien) and inevitably the myths woven by us, though they contain error, will also reflect a splintered fragment of the true light, the eternal truth that is with God. Indeed only by myth-making, only by becoming a 'sub-creator' and inventing stories, can Man ascribe to the state of perfection that he knew before the Fall. Our myths may be misguided, but they steer us however shakily towards the true harbour, while materialistic 'progress' leads only to a yawning abyss and the Iron Crown of the power of evil."

In fact, in his essay on fairy stories, Tolkien suggests two factors in his own life which led him to the fantasy mode: "A real taste for fairy-stories was wakened by philology on the threshold of manhood, and quickened to full life by war." Scholarship and war fill *Lord*, and it is interesting that the forces of good fellowship have prepared for this war which ushers in *Eucatastrophe* by scholarly pursuits and even philological researches.

Tolkien insists in his essay that fantasy, in this best sense, informed by learning, language, and human struggle, "is, I think, not a lower but a higher form of Art, indeed the most nearly pure form, and so (when achieved) the most potent." The divided fellowship now fully mobilized in the great sweep of war begins its last maneuvers. For Aragorn, accompanied by Gimli and Legolas, this means a mission of death and rebirth, and Aragorn resolves to follow the words of an ancient seer and pass through the Door to the Paths of the Dead. Eowyn pronounces a kind of final benediction: "And he has passed into the shadows from which none have returned. . . .He is gone." Theoden relays the ancient legends which describe the shadow land, where "the Dead keep it, until the time comes." Baldor asks the obvious: "And when will that time be?" The answer is merely another question from Eomer: "But how shall a man discover whether that time be come or no, save by daring the Door?" Merry, who has remained with Theoden, casts his thoughts over all he has heard: "The Paths of the Dead? What does all this mean? They have all left me now. They have all gone to some doom: Gandalf and Pippin to war in the East; and Sam and Frodo to Mordor; and Strider and Legolas and Gimli to the Paths of the Dead. But my turn will come soon enough. . . ."

The "turn" of that last phrase does arrive quickly. Theoden and his company, including Merry, march off to join the war. Time itself appears to be cyclic and recurrent, turning, wheeling, like the narrative as it turns from character to character. Chapter 4, "The Siege of Gondor," returns to Pippin, this time being awakened by Gandalf: " 'What is the time?' said Pippin yawning. 'Past the second hour,' said Gandalf. 'Time to get up and make yourself presentable. . . .' " Pippin is armed in black and silver, and prepares to face the final battle. Tolkien again gives us a glimpse of Pippin's introspection: "Already it seemed years to Pippin since he had sat there before in some half-forgotten time when he had still been a hobbit, a lighthearted wanderer touched little by the perils he had passed through. Now he was one small soldier in a city preparing for a great assault, clad in the proud but sombre manner of the Tower of Guard." Only a novel of Proustian scope can depict time in this way: vast, cyclic, overwhelming in the changes and the circumstances it haunts.

Encircled by a "ring of foes," the seven-ringed city of Gondor falls under siege. And the most terrible weapon of the Lord of the Dark Tower is that thematic antithesis which cannot compensate loss; "dread and despair" are the exact antitheses of memory and hope. The dark forces harness the destructive powers of alienated nature in the image of evil technology: "Great engines crawled across the field; and in the midst was a huge ram, great as a forest-tree a hundred feet in length, swinging on mighty chains. Long had it been forged in the dark smithies of Mordor, and its hideous head, founded of black steel, was shaped in the likeness of a ravening wolf. . . ." With this evil engine and "words of power and terror to rend both heart and stone" hammering at the Gates of Gondor, the entrance gives way: "As if stricken by some blasting spell. . .there was a flash of searing lightning, and the doors tumbled in riven fragments to the ground." The image of lightning, complex and pervasive in this great war, is a force of sudden power and swift destruction. It is energy in its purest, most startling, visible form. Morally neutral, that power can be turned to good or ill. Here, linked to dread and despair and the blackness of the weapons (like the blackness of the thunderclouds), it is clearly not a force for clarity and enlightenment. The Black Rider gives out deadly laughter from an unseen mouth and shouts that the time is his—that we are witnessing a battle for possession, and that he will possess not only the city (space) but the temporal plane as well: "Old fool! Old fool! This is my hour."

The epithet of "fool" takes on increasing importance in the crucial battle scenes, and as the word gets tossed around, applied to Gandalf as well as to Sam and Frodo, we begin to hear echoes of the traditional "fool for Christ," the fool who is more deeply wise than the wise man. The reality which survives and is victorious is deeper than the surface, more enduring than mere appearances. We have been prepared for this sense that reality lies beyond appearance by the fact that those apparently dead can be reborn, and by the fact that the dark forces are essentially invisible, and that the very Rings which are supposed to confer power actually rob the wearer of all visible substance. Tolkien immediately reminds us that despite appearances, time cannot be owned or claimed for any earthly force. It moves of its own, with a dimension and a reality untouched by claims of ownership: "And in that moment, away behind in some courtyard of the City, a cock crowed. Still and clear he crowed, recking nothing of wizardry or war, welcoming only the morning that in the sky far above the shadows of death was coming with the dawn."

The style of writing in this final book is Tolkien's most serious, elevated, and poetic. Its formal cadences give a measured and ordered development to the chaotic and sprawling events it depicts. Repetition and inverted syntax are skillfully combined for rhetorical effect in, for instance, the passage that announces the entrance of the Dark Lord into Gondor: "In rode the Lord of the Nazgul. A great black shape against the fires beyond he loomed up, grown to a vast menace of despair. In rode the Lord of Nazgul, under the archway that no enemy ever yet had passed, and all fled before his face." As Tolkien said of the author of *Beowulf*, the high tone, the sense of dignity alone are evidence of the presence of a mind lofty and thoughtful. Even in the direst threat of despair we are unaware of a terrible beauty in the language and rhythm of the writing; we are aware of the creative (subcreative) power at work in the very face of this Dark Lord, beyond the touch of his destruction.

This high style, which would have seemed so terribly out of place in the lightly-told *Hobbit*, has been gradually built up and prepared. One of the finest examples of it, in fact, occurs in the description of the Dark Lord's death, and Chapter 5 serves in a vastly shortened form to recapitulate that stylistic development. Tolkien describes the creation of the universe in terms of music in the "Valaquenta," and the metaphor is tacitly a part of the rhetorical development and crescendo throughout his writings. The celebration, elevation, and perpetuation through song is part of the thematic fabric of the tale, from Tom Bombadil to the stately hymn of the eagle's victory at the end of the book: "Sing now, ye people of the Tower of Anor,/for the Realm of Sauron is ended for ever." The linguistic orchestration of Chapter 5 is a joy to experience. The beginning is ordinary, matter-of-fact, almost trivial. We set out psychologically close to Merry: "It was dark and Merry could see nothing as he lay on the ground rolled in a blanket; yet though the night was airless and windless, all about him hidden trees were sighing softly. . . . a sound like faint drums in the wooded hills and mountain-steps." The drum beats throb and build, in a symphonic and ominous presence behind the plain little hobbit rolled up in a blanket.

Several paragraphs later, "Merry wanted somebody to talk to": colloquial, slight, and in keeping with the smallness of hobbits rather than the cosmic events of the high style. As the nearby armies mobilize and people loom around him, Merry listens to the drums and feels lonely, until a figure stumbles over him and curses the tree-roots. "I am not a tree-root, Sir," says Merry, "nor a bag, but a bruised hobbit." In this insignificant comedy we hearken back to the earlier events of the book. Merry is about to become a great hero, playing his part in the slaying of the Dark Lord himself, but his tiny unimportance is dramatically depicted here. His comment about the "tree-root" is literally appropriate for the occasion, but symbolically important as well, since he is setting himself apart from the Ents who had conquered the Dark Lord's deputy in the Tower battle. The reference to "bag," of course, takes us back to Bag End, and to Baggins, as does the whole bit of comic relief in this "Andante" section. Elhelm, the marshal who has stumbled over him, gives him orders before this battle that comment upon his rolled-up blanket, his constant protection within Gandalf's cloak, and the other sacks and packets Merry has been inside: "Pack yourself up, Master Bag!" By the swift end of the chapter, Merry's heart "beat slowly," taking the somber tempo of the throbbing drums, and "Time seemed poised in uncertainty" until Merry himself comes round: "Then suddenly Merry felt it at last, beyond doubt: a change. Wind was in his face! Light was glimmering. . . . in the South the clouds could be dimly seen. . . . morning lay beyond them. But at that same moment there was a flash, as if lightning had sprung from the earth beneath the City." And suddenly the language rolls like the great sweep of a grand symphony, like the stately elevation of the King James Bible: "For morning came, morning and a wind from the sea; and darkness was removed, and the hosts of Mordor wailed, and terror took them, and they fled, and died, and the hoofs of wrath rode over them. And then all the host of Rohan burst into song, and they sang as they slew, for the joy of battle was on them, and the sound of their singing that was fair and terrible came even to the City." The lengthy syntax resounds with repetition, in marked contrast to the staccato exchanges of the early portions of this chapter. The sentences are long, stately, linked and joined by conjunctions. One thing flows into the next, and it is all one utterance, not divided, lonely, isolated, rolled up in a blanket, stumbled and kicked in darkness, but celebrated, harmonious and grandiose in the singing light of day.

Appropriate use of inverted syntax is most evident in the description of the Dark Lord's downfall. First there is the irony that Merry and Dernhelm stand for the forces of good in this final battle. Dernhelm (who is in fact Eowyn, Eomund's daughter) had been forbidden from the battle, and when Merry was told not to go, it was Eowyn/Dernhelm who brought him, sharing the same horse. With Theoden down, Merry and Eowyn face the lord of carrion who calls again: "Thou fool. No living man may hinder me!" But, in the manner of the Shakespearean Birnham Wood device, the lord faces "no man," but a hobbit and a woman and, in fact, he has been fooled by their appearance. As Merry faces the master of evil, "suddenly the slow-kindled courage of his race awoke." The actions of the Dark Lord are depicted in ordinary subject-verb-object order: "The Black Captain. . . heeded him no more than a worm in the mud."; "swiftly fell down upon Eowyn"; "he let fall his mace"; "He raised his mace to kill"; "his stroke went wide." Eowyn's actions are first elevated by inverted order object-subject-verb: "A swift stroke she dealt, skilled and deadly. The outstretched neck she clove asunder, and the hewn head fell like a stone." The object accomplished, the syntax returns to rightful order: "Backward she sprang as the huge shape crashed to ruin, vast wings outspread, crumpled on the earth; and with its fall the shadow passed away. A light fell about her, and her hair shone in the sunrise." The inverted syntax places the object first in the sentence, as it is in the hearts and minds of the heroes, and the inverted order has the effect of elevating what appear to be minor characters by the noble objects they hold before them. The final sentence which describes Eowyn's last swordthrust achieves a different sort of effect, suspending the subject and the object in action. The sentence begins with gerundial verb forms which leave us hanging, until the final thrust is brought home: "Then tottering, struggling up, with her last strength she drove her sword between crown and mantle, as the great shoulders bowed before her. The sword broke sparkling into many shards. The crown rolled away with a clang. Eowyn fell forward upon her fallen foe." With the concluding of the action, positions in the real world have been inverted. The Dark Lord has bowed to the uncrowned woman; the woman has subdued this foe even to placing her body on top of his, and as the very substance of the Dark Lord dissolves, it is clear that time itself has given way and a new age is about to begin: "And a cry went up into the shuddering air, and faded to a shrill wailing, passing with the wind, a voice bodiless and thin that died, and was swallowed up and was never heard again in that age of this world."

The fifth book concludes with renewal in the houses of healing, where Aragorn, the new king, can restore the fallen to health by a laying on of hands. The recoveries of Merry, Eowyn, and Faramir promise further rebirth under this new ruler: and Tolkien demonstrates that each of these have been reborn with spiritual and personal depth. Eowyn learns a new understanding of love; Faramir deeper in knowledge and love; Merry in love and priorities. Merry's eloquent statement provides an opportunity for Tolkien to state firmly and clearly one of the messages of his work: "It is best to love first what you are fitted to love—you must start somewhere and have some roots, and the soil of the Shire is deep. Still there are things deeper and higher; and not a gaffer could tend his garden in what he calls peace but for them, whether he knows about them or not. I am glad that I know about them a little. But I don't know why I am talking like this," he lamely apologizes and asks for a pipe for a smoke."

This section of the book, in fact, abounds in explicit thematic statements. This serves well, for the central decisive battles toward which the whole narration has been directed, proceed in rapid order, building in turn to an even larger final climax. Again and again we pass through this sequence of struggle, apparent death and rebirth. The episode of healing is quickly followed by "The Last Debate," where Gandalf helps the companions and the reader understand that the struggle is not yet over: "Hardly has our strength sufficed to beat off the first great assault. The next will be greater. This war then is without final hope. . . . Victory cannot be achieved by arms."

Like the epic *Beowulf* which he so greatly admired, Tolkien's *Lord* gives us a modern fusion of Norse and Christian sensibilities. In his famous essay on Beowulf, "The Monsters and the Critics," Tolkien reflects that "One of the most potent elements in that fusion is the Northern Courage: the theory of courage, which is the great contribution of early Northern literature." Nordic myth presented the idea that real courage could only be found in fighting on the right side against hopeless odds. The same tradition held that the right side will ultimately lose out to Chaos and Unreason—"mythically, the monsters," Tolkien explains—and he points out that pagan English and Norse imaginations agreed about "this vision of the final defeat of the humane (and of the divine made in its image), and in the essential hostility of the gods and heroes on the one hand and the monsters on the other." The poet in this view" sees that all glory (or as we might say 'culture' or 'civilization') ends in night," and that this mirrors another fact which requires courage: "Each man and all men, and all their works shall die." It is from this base that they so profoundly admire "defeated valour in this world." Tolkien admires the strength of this position: "It is the strength of the northern mythological imagination that it faced this problem, put the monsters in the centre, gave them victory but no honour, and found a potent but terrible solution in naked will and courage. . . . So potent is it, that while the older southern imagination has faded for ever into literary ornament, the northern has power, as it were, to revive its spirit even in our own times."

In his sustained series of climactic battles, Tolkien is at pains to present the hopelessness of the situation. From another perspective, the situation is highlighted with the frequent references to the characters we know to be the heroes as "fools." Tolkien wishes to establish conditions which give rise to contests of naked will and to profound courage; and then he lifts us within the Christian perspective through a death to rebirth. This is of course conveyed most deeply and centrally in the main plot—this greatest work of the world, the One Ring, must be destroyed so that the work of the world can be renewed and reborn.

As they deliberate their assault on the very fortress of Sauron, Gandalf demonstrates again his ability to understand the workings of the dark mind, while the good intentions can never be known to Sauron. He concludes: "We must walk open-eyed into that trap, with courage, but small hope for ourselves." For Tolkien, however, that small hope is not equivalent to certain defeat. His Norse sympathies are fused to the hope in fools and little children of Christianity: "That we should ride with seven thousands, scarce as many as the vanguard of its army in the days of its power, to assail the mountains and the impenetrable gate of the Black Land! So might a child threaten a mail-clad knight with a bow of string and green willow!" At the end of this very chapter the tiny hobbit saves Beregond by killing the monstrous troll-chief before he falls himself "away into a great darkness."

Book Six begins with Sam Gamgee regaining consciousness, uncertain "how long he had lain there," but slowly reorienting himself regarding his mission. It is clear to him now that he must rescue his master, and to do this he must confront the Tower of Girith Ungol. Here the tower as an image of technological man is rendered even more explicit, and Sam's conquest is accomplished inside a tower-as-body. Before he approaches, he looks it over, and the narrow windows at the top seem "like small red eyes." Within the very province of the eye that has attempted to pierce though all the maneuverings of the fellowship, Sam moves unseen and accidentally toward the rescue of Frodo. His heart and will are in the right place, and if his judgment is not the keenest, he still survives on instinct.

As he puts on the Ring to try to learn more about his circumstances, he finds the "things of this world seemed thin and vague." He is aware of the "Eye of Mordor, searching, trying to pierce the shadows that it had made for its own defence, but which now hindered it in its unquiet and doubt." The forces of darkness clearly do not know themselves any better than they know the forces of good. Sam, in marked contrast, is largely untouched by the symbols and trappings of power which do not suit his ordinary nature. He is guided by two factors: "love of his master," and "his plain hobbit-sense": "He knew in the core of his heart that he was not large enough to bear such a burden, even if such visions were not a mere cheat to betray him. The one small garden of a free gardenery was all his need and due, not a garden swollen to a realm; his own hands to use, not the hands of others to command."

Sam is literally and figuratively the good gardener. He rejects temptation and his only interest in the tower is in leaving it. In fact, the tower, like Babel, has been struck by chaos and confusion. It is such a hodge-podge of voices that even Sam is mistaken for Frodo, and he is fortuitously reunited with his master because of this very confusion. The Orcs have been hit by their most dramatic case of conflict and anger, a quality of dissent shown clearly and consistently to be part of their nature, as it is truly part of all who lust for possession and dominance. They make their escape from the tower because the forces of Mordor have consumed themselves in confusion, and they finally elude the gates as they entered them, through the borrowed power of the Elven-glass of Galadriel. As Sam brings forth the phial, the illumination is described in the familiar metaphor of lightning, but it is now sustained and altered, "so that all the shadowy court was lit with a dazzling radiance like lightning; but it remained steady and did not pass." Sam's faithfulness and steady nature bring them through the tower episode, and Sam is quick to sense in the next chapter that a change is in the making: "Something's happening. He's not having it all his own way. His darkness is breaking up out in the world there." Microcosm mirrors macrocosm: there is a strange synchronous action in the final events which shows time in yet another light. Tolkien reminds us of Theoden's death and the events of the war already narrated, but the connection of the lightning Sam sees and the victory they have just won with the light of Galadriel is too apparent to be missed.

Sam provides the strength and confidence for the last leg of the journey, and Tolkien makes a point of describing his changing condition. He follows Sam's thoughts, allowing them humorously commonplace and random directions as well as more profound and difficult paths. Even as Sam thinks of the hopeless task before them, and the thought finally hits that "There could be no return," Tolkien shows Sam's nature capable of enduring past hope: "But even as hope died in Sam, or seemed to die, it was turned to a new strength. Sam's plain hobbit-face grew stern, almost grim, as the will hardened in him, and he felt through all his limbs a thrill, as if he was turning into some creature of stone and steel that neither despair nor weariness nor endless barren miles could subdue." With this new strength of will, Sam resolves to see his master safely through the quest. He decides he will carry Frodo, if that should become necessary, and with the ring weighing ever heavier on Frodo, this becomes a matter of increasing likelihood.

Here Tolkien turns his final use of lightning to a new and much more human purpose. Like the lightning that first struck its appeal in the hobbit's comfortable hole, this new sense is unexpected. Sam sits down and "To his surprise he felt tired but *lighter*, and his head seemed *clear* again." The new kind of lightning releases the load of the heavy burden of the Ring because it stems from a selfless dedication and faithfulness radically different from the oppressive power plays of Mordor. Everywhere around Mount Doom the sky is black, and the power of the dark forces can be seen in "a shimmer of lightnings under the black skies," but Sam's head is clear, and the lightning is a surprising reservoir of strength in an ordinary and humble little body. As in the accidental victory at the Orc Tower, this lightness is a remarkable attunement of various outside forces. It is a gift of grace freely given, and Tolkien links it to the cosmic symbol of light: "And slowly the light of the unseen Sun filtered down into the shadows where the hobbits lay."

Tolkien has prepared us for what happens next, though we have never thought of it consciously. The burden of the Ring has become such that Frodo himself can scarcely move. He slowly lifts himself to the knees and begins to inch forward when Sam finally determines to carry him: "Sam staggered to his feet; and then to his amazement he felt the burden light." Here is perhaps the most unexpected "lightning from a clear sky." We have known that both Bilbo and Frodo tended to become stretched and thin under the influence of the Ring, as though they were undergoing disembodiment. It therefore makes wonderful good sense that this thin physical frame should be light to the faithful Sam. They make it to their destination by discarding every unnecessary possession, by metaphorically lightening their burdens, by discarding any desire save one—the giving up of the Ring. At the time when they are at their furthest extreme from hobbit-hole comfort, when their strength is not sufficient to their cause, a final lightening of their load comes as an unexpected blessing. When strength and will have stood their test in the face of the hopeless defeat (the Northern courage), Tolkien allows a final gift of grace which makes that strength suffice.   The pace quickens as time after time Sam thinks they are at the end of their journey, only to find another twist of events or renewed strength to go on. Gollum returns and nearly catches them off guard, but Frodo is fired by the dark power of the Ring itself to fight to protect his ownership, and he thrusts Gollum away toward Sam with the threat that should the creature ever touch the ring again he will be thrown into the Crack of Doom. Sam faces Gollum, holding him at swordpoint while Frodo goes on to enter the mountainside, but Sam, moved by something "deep in his heart," does not kill Gollum. He sends him away, and turns to follow his master into a darkness so deep that even the phial of Galadriel is unable to shine there. Sudden flames from the Crack of Doom reveal Frodo, true to his hobbit nature as "thief," deciding to keep the Ring for himself after all, and he disappears as he puts it on his finger. That act shakes the Power of Barad-dur, since suddenly the controlling Ring has been claimed at last by a master. Then the end turns again for a final time, as Gollum leaps from the shadows and literally bites the ring off of Frodo's finger before toppling into the Crack of Doom in a mad fit. Gollum's possessive drive has turned him far from his own best nature in a phrase Tolkien uses twice in the space of two paragraphs, into " a mad thing." Desiring this object so absolutely, Gollum becomes in turn an object, a thing, lost in the flames of the material world where the power of individual will has been destroyed by greed. Frodo concludes the chapter with a speech of "forgiveness" for Gollum, who has served a good purpose after all, just as Gandalf predicted. Even Frodo, despite the loss of a finger, declares "The Quest is achieved, and now all is over. I am glad you are here with me. Here at the end of all things, Sam."

There is irony in the speech, of course, for there still remain more than 100 pages in the main body of Tolkien's narrative, and following that, well over 100 pages of notes and appendices. The end is really not here yet; in Sam's words, we have still not had an "end of ends." There is even some doubt about whether we have witnessed the real climax, for the following chapter offers other major events which might count for the honor. The climax is sustained into the next chapter, picking up where Pippin lost consciousness at the end of Book V. On the Field of Cormallen we watch the effects of the trembling of Barad-dur. The moment is re-played from another perspective, and Gandalf announces "The realm of Sauron is ended. . . . The Ring-bearer has fulfilled his Quest." This literary re-play marks the end of Tolkien's manipulations of time; from this point to the end of his book events proceed chronologically. Henceforth, the year will begin on this day, March 25, the day on which Sauron fell (and in the Catholic calendar, the first of the Annunciation).

If the crucial dimension of this final book is, as I have suggested, time, one thing Tolkien makes quite clear is that time does not ever stop on Middle Earth. We watch the ending of one age, but that means the beginning of another. Though the ring is itself destroyed, the cyclic time frame which defines Middle Earth continues, and Tolkien's story continues to immerse us in the new chronology. Part of the theme is in this volume's title work, "Return": time now will turn anew, but it will continue nonetheless. The new age will mean new challenges and new losses; the book does not stop at a point which would lead the reader to believe that a final end has actually been reached. We return to Bilbo's birthday, to the Shire and to Bag End, but still it is not over. We find that the forces of evil have not been eliminated; Saruman and Wormtongue are still on the prowl, causing destruction in the Shire; but Gandalf explains that time has accomplished growth, if not a final solution: "I am not coming to the Shire. You must settle its affairs yourselves; that is what you have been trained for. Do you not understand? My time is over: it is no longer my task to set things to rights, nor to help folk to do so. And as for you, my dear friends, you will need no help. You are grown up now. Grown indeed very high; among the great you are, and I have no longer any fear at all for any of you." Merry and Pippin, who have grown literally as well as figuratively, and Sam, are indeed able to "scour" the Shire and set it right. One of the saving aspects of the cycles of time is the wonderful growth in these characters we have witnessed—and the growth from the *Hobbit*, practically a children's story, to this clearly adult, mature, and far-ranging final volume. The readers, along with the hobbits, have been eased into a "grown-up" attitude of responsible action which should be able to accept the constant struggle in time, and the sense of loss one always must face within it.

Sam and the other hobbits set about repairing the shire, dragging down the ugly housing, planting and tending the land again. Sam remembers the gift of Galadriel and finds a silver nut and magic dust which creates rapid and lush growth "as if time was in a hurry and wished to make one year do for twenty." Most of the damage to the shire is repaired in this last gift from an earlier age, and with the thriving of the new mallorn tree in the restored shire, those remnants of the third age are fully replaced. Elrond, Galadriel, Gandalf, Frodo, and Bilbo board a ship and sail away into an unknown distance, largely unnoticed. Despite the pain of this final separation we are prepared for and can accept it, like Sam, with a painful simplicity. The book ends with close focus on Sam and his family. The final *return* is to family fellowship: "And Rose drew him in, and set him in his chair, and put little Elanor upon his lap. He drew a deep breath. 'Well, I'm back.' he said."

Despite the richly colloquial and homey quality of the final words, the conclusion of *Lord* is rendered in a formal style, highly conjunctive, rhythmical, and stately. Consider the departure by ship already cited: "Then Frodo kissed Merry and Pippin, and last of all Sam, and went aboard; and the sails were drawn up, and the wind blew, and slowly the ship slipped away down the long grey firth; and the light of the glass of Galadriel that Frodo bore glimmered and was lost." The word order is active declarative, subject-verb-object, in the first independent clause: following the semi-colon the action becomes passive as the major actors disappear. Appropriate sentence structures are complemented by skillful rhetoric. The light which glimmers and then vanishes is a common rhetorical trope of *synecdoche*, a part used to stand for a whole, Frodo's light is a part of the light of the Silmaril, in turn a part of the light of the mingled Two Trees; it stands for the whole promise of the third great age which is now gone, casting even the rhetorical device into a symbolic mode. Tolkien makes constant use of classical rhetorical figures, but increasingly elaborate schemes and tropes appear in the final volume of *The Lord*. By the way of rhetorical schemes, *anaphora* (the repetition of a word or phrase at the openings of successive clauses), and *chiasmus* (a pattern of criss-crossing a syntactic, or a reversal of syntax for a similar effect) are among the most common. There is conscious care for compatibility of figure and genre as well.

The great battle scenes are rendered with an epic scope, and the narrative includes pure epic similes which could have come straight out of Milton or even Homer: "As when death smites the swollen brooding thing that inhabits their crawling hill and holds them all in sway, ants will wander witless and purposeless and then feebly die, so the creatures of Sauron, Orc or troll or beast spell-enslaved, ran hither and thither mindless. . . ." Chapter Four, "The Field of Cormallen," begins with what is very nearly a classic epic hexameter: "All about the hills the hosts of Mordor raged," and within his prose Tolkien utilizes meters reminiscent of epic and narrative poetry in both Northern and Southern traditions. Internal rhyme and alliteration contribute to its poetic quality. In the following typical example I have divided Tolkien's prose sentence to indicate the rhythms more clearly: "The onslaught of Mordor/broke like a wave/on the beleaguered hills,/voices roaring like a tide/amid the wreck and clash of arms."

Sounds and words have played an important role throughout The Lord, but they attain a height of classic fullness with the climax of the narrative. The downfall of Sauron is rendered in words which echo and imitate the sounds they describe in an onomatopoaeic fashion, at the same time that the description of the destruction itself is calmly enshrined in a cadenced and balanced syntax; note that the three "now" phrases in the first part of the following clause are precisely echoed in the three phrases of consonance and assonance which conclude the sentence: "And from far away, now dim, now growing, now mounting to the clouds, there came a drumming rumble, a roar, a long echoing roll of ruinous noise." The cacophonous sounds of Sauron's end serve as appropriate counterbalance to a creation of the world through music, as told in "Ainulindale." The minstrel who hushes the celebrants with his clear words projects an image of transcendence, of a celebration in language beyond antithesis: "And he sang to them, now in the Elven-tongue, now in the speech of the West, until their hearts, wounded with sweet words, overflowed, and their joy was like swords, and they passed in thought out to regions where pain and delight flow together and tears are the very wine of blessedness."

Many of the greatest characters in Tolkien's tales tend to become invisible— to disappear finally into story, into language, into song. And as the characters become "lighter," in the concluding understanding of "lightning," the style of the fiction becomes heavier, weightier. One can see the process in the various titles scrawled on the big red book Frodo presents to Sam; they range from the trivial and trite beginning: "My Diary" and "My Unexpected Journey," to the final dignified "The Downfall of the Lord of the Rings and the Return of the King." A clear, compelling tale appears as the actors in that chronicle disappear. Frodo tells Sam as much when he hands him the book: "I tried to save the Shire, and it has been saved, but not for me. It must often be so, Sam, when things are in danger: someone has to give them up, lose them, so that others may keep them." Frodo predicts Sam will be the most famous gardener in history, and he charges him with what will perhaps be an even more important job of caretaking: "And you will read things out of the Red Book, and keep alive the memory of the age that is gone, so that people will remember the Great Danger and so love their beloved land all the more."

IV. THE SILMARILLION

In a sense, *The Silmarillion* is like a continuation of the appendices to *The Lord of the Rings*. It is a difficult body of material, a collection of myths which form both the beginning and the end of the Tolkien canon. The volume includes, in addition to the title work, "Ainulindale," "Valaquenta," "Akallabeth," and "Of the Rings of Power and the Third Age." The collection is sensitively edited and organized by Christopher Tolkien. It begins with Eru, "the One," who propounds themes of music for the offspring of his thought and generates the universal pattern of creation; it ends where *The Lord* ends, with the story of the sailing of Gandalf, Frodo, and the others: "In the twilight of autumn it sailed out of Mithlond, until the seas of the Bent World fell away beneath it, and the winds of the round sky troubled it no more, and borne upon the high airs above the mists of the world it passed into the Ancient West." After this ascension of substance into air, a process of "lightning" again, we are left with music, the way it all began; the book ends acknowledging the wealth "of story and of song."

There are many stories and episodes in the *Silmarillion*; in fact, too many to discuss here in detail. The structure is neither that of novel or epic, but imitates the form of various fragmentary surviving ancient manuscripts and related cycles of tales. Its style and structure are unique in twentieth century English literature.

To date, the most perceptive approach to what he calls "Tolkien's music" in *The Silmarillion* comes in a brief note by Donald G. Keller in the Nov.-Dec., 1977 issue of *Fantasiae*, the monthly newsletter of the Fantasy Association. Keller offers "Preliminary Remarks on Style in *The Silmarillion*." He points out that it would be easy to notice a stylistic evolution in Tolkien's writing, from the children's book through the "English-popular-novel tone of the early parts" of *Lord* to the "epic high style of the latter parts to the mythic high style of *The Silmarillion*." But he also observes that *The Silmarillion* was written first, that the elevated rhetoric both preceded and followed the more ordinary styles. Keller defends the thesis that "the high style was his natural style from the first, and he adopted the low style to make his work more marketable."

While I don't agree with those who would term the high style "juvenile excrescence he never got rid of," neither can I term it "natural." It is highly cultivated, and "artificial" in the best sense. This formal approach to style seems to have appealed to Tolkien from the first—a style full of artifice, invention, and careful consistency—and his choice of it seems related to two other points Keller makes: "Tolkien was a trained scholar, and his profession made him familiar with the epic and legendary literature that preceded the novel, and all his writings show that he was far more at home with them. The best parts of *LOTR* (the Moria and Lothlorien episodes, for example) have supernatural and mythic depth. His talent is macrocosmic rather than microcosmic. *LOTR* is not a novel, but a medieval-style romance, a secondary epic; the *Silmarillion* is primary epic." *The Silmarillion* is "primary epic" in concept and in style, though not in form, character, or narrative approach. In any case it served as a primary source for *The Lord*, a work which conforms more closely to many of the categories of epic form.

One of the most remarkable things about Tolkien's fiction is the sustained coherence of his world; *The Silmarillion* is the basis for this integrity. It is also like an "appendix" in that once it is appended to a reading of the earlier work, it deepens and extends the entire *ouvre*. Reading *Silmarillion* one begins to understand the kind of document the Red Book would have been, and how different in both form and style these chronicles are from the modern popular novel.

The Red Book, *The Silmarillion*, and the Primary Epic differ from other literary works in purporting to narrate historical origins (events which have already taken place); they constitute a subcreated *mythos* offering a coherent reading of the universe, its laws and powers, and man's place in it. In effect, *The Silmarillion* is a modern scripture. It figuratively shows the origins of good and evil, the conflict and loss since the beginning, and suggests man's place in the continuing battles when he inherits the weight of responsibility at the end of the Third Age. Like *Gilgamesh* or *The Bible*, the macrocosmic scope of Tolkien's final work affords limitless opportunity for interpretation and commentary.

The Silmarillion is similar to a Primary Epic in its presentation of events, tales, myths from many sources—Elven Sources, the Red Book, etc. This is part of the fiction, but Christopher Tolkien mentions in his Foreword that his father came to conceive the book "as a compilation, a compendous narrative, made long afterwards from sources of great diversity (poems, and annals, and oral tales) that had survived in agelong traditon." It is like a Primary Epic in having been formed through a version of the oral tradition—Tolkien's telling and reading the stories aloud to his family and to the Inklings. On the other hand, the book is like a secondary epic in that it actually is not a compilation, but the invention of a single mind; it is actually not composed in an oral tradition, but has been written, revised, and edited by both Tolkien and his son. It resembles secondary epic in having tighter form and purpose and more unified symbolic structures than a work by multiple authors. It is unlike classical epic in using what Moses Hadas has referred to as "the apocalyptic technique" stemming from a later period, and informed particularly in Tolkien's case by Christian sources. While the *Silmarillion* stories did evolve over Tolkien's lifetime, they have been shaped as much by literary as oral factors. Yet, like the epics, they employ elevated language, great battle scenes, division into Books, displays of superhuman powers, and extended similes.

In addition, Tolkien has chosen to use strong elements of Northern mythologies in shaping his stories and his epic form. (The name "Gandalf" as well as other dwarf names were taken from the Elder Edda, for instance.) The Norse sagas are considered yet another form of epic—what has been called the "epic of growth"—collections of lyrics, poems, or ballads composed by different authors at different times, all dealing with related events. This seems very close indeed to the material involved in the "compendious narrative" Tolkien felt he was writing. The Icelandic Niblung story and the Finnish Kalevala are examples of the older form. By incorporating various epic traditions and types into one form—and one, moreover, which closely adheres to the requirements Aristotle prescribed for the epic in his *Poetics*, including a unity of action—Tolkien devises a unique form of fantasy writing.

The episodes collected in *The Silmarillion* are almost entirely action. There is little character development, little familiar description, and practically no psychological exploration. It is an "epic of return" written in the high mimetic mode (to use Northrop Frye's classification). Its scope is larger than *The Lord*, more detached and elemental, encompassing an enormous range of knowledge and history. At the end of *The Lord* Sam Gamgee returns to his bride and to restored nature, society and law, the proper master of his house and mayor in perpetuity—the return of Odysseus. Gandalf and Frodo return after the great war and the overthrow of Mordor to assume responsibility for the death of the Third Age and the beginning of the New Age—the return of Aeneas with the downfall of Troy and the establishment of the New Troy. *The Silmarillion* repeats and contains both of these patterns. Like *The Bible* it is an encyclopedic epic; Miltonic and Biblical parallels are profuse. Tolkien's Christian perspective is evident in style and theme: and his depiction of return is an affirmation of rebirth. He does not leave his narrative at the brink of apocalypse, but follows the path beyond it.

The history of light in *The Silmarillion* is once again a cyclic tale of recovery, escape, consolation. The tale *begins* at the *beginning*, more like the *Bible* than like the classical epic, *in medias res*. It begins with Genesis ("Ainulindale" and "Valaquenta") and proceeds from the first creation to the second, with Aule making the Dwarves, and Feanor making the Silmarils. Finally, we are faced with destruction, fall, conflict, and darkness: Melkor and Avathar conspire to seize the Silmarils and destroy the light of the Two Trees: "The Light failed; but the Darkness that followed seemed not a lack of a thing with being of its own: for it was indeed made by malice out of light, and it had power to pierce the eye, and to enter heart and mind, and strangle the very will." The anti-creative spirit of this loss is reinforced by the antithesis of the harmonious music with which creation began, for Melkor/Morgoth, nearly trapped in the web of his own deceits by his ally Ungoliant, gives forth a horrible cry: "The cry of Morgoth in that hour was the greatest and most dreadful that was ever heard in the northen world; the mountains shook, and the earth trembled, and rocks were riven asunder." It is a cry of black destruction. It is the irrevocable Fall repeated at the end of *The Silmarillion*: "Yet the lies that Melkor, the mighty and accursed, Morgoth Bauglir, the Power of Terror and of Hate, sowed in the hearts of Elves and Men are a seed that does not die and cannot be destroyed; and ever and anon it sprouts anew, and will bear dark fruit even unto the latest days."

Within this fallen creation Men are given a special role, a role toward which all of Tolkien's writing leads. The New Age will be the age of Men, but the fullness of the adventures in this age are not yet known. *The Silmarillion* cannot tell of the ultimate fate of men: "The fate of Men after death, maybe, is not in the hands of the Valar, nor was all foretold in the Music of the Ainur." Men have the "virtue to shape their life, amid the powers and chances of the world, beyond the Music of the Ainur, which is as fate to all things else." And Tolkien shows in the very process of creation a special freely-given gift of redemption, as well as free will given to Men: "But Iluvatar knew that Men, being set amid the turmoils of the powers of the world, would stray often, and would not use their gifts in harmony; and he said: 'These too in their time shall find that all that they do redounds at the end only to the glory of my work.' "

"In their time," echoes the temporal emphasis in the final volume of *The Lord*, when we are brought up to the age of Men and left with that time in which to find direction, shape and 'glory' for ourselves. *The Silmarillion* fills in the mythic background of *The Lord* with other rich patterns of aspiration and loss and recovery. The splendid tale of Beren and Luthien is one of the most appealing. It also establishes an archetypal precedent for Frodo's loss of his finger trying to destroy the Ring, for Beren loses a hand recovering the single Silmaril. But the main point about *The Silmarillion* is that it is a Bible, an encyclopedic epic of return which shows us ways of living with loss and the pain of recovery. Nearly contradictory to the theme of loss in the tales is the medium itself, the great wealth of mythic and archetypal invention, creation, recovery, which *The Silmarillion* contains. The scope and magnitude of this invention, the range of imagination, can inspire and reassure us in the midst of deprivation, and raise our own age (the Age of Man) by the power of invention: it is possible, Tolkien assures us, to construct a dream of coherence—a total, beautiful subcreation.

The Silmarillion is a crown of light, a properly inspiring testament to be returned to and reread with growing pleasure. It is both the beginning and the culmination of Tolkien's subcreation. Unlike many other fantasy writers, Tolkien is reluctant to discard the worlds he has made in order to invent new ones. He affirms a continuous and uninterrupted story, a unity of existence which can be illuminated by a parallel, coherent subcreative process. Like music and light, the creative imagination itself is, strictly speaking, without substance. Yet in the literary forms he has invented Tolkien allows this imagination to shine forth brightly; and if it does not recreate the reality of the light from the original Two Trees, it at least keeps alive the memory of their beauty. All this is ideal subcreation, an affirmation of the gift given Men in *The Silmarillion*, the "virtue to shape their life, amid the powers and chances of the world." Tolkien's unified and illuminating literary inventions rest on a simple lesson from the greater Bible: "Ye are the light of the world. . . Let your light so shine before men that they may see your good works, and glorify your Father which is in heaven."

V. SOME CLOSING REMARKS

In another Milford Series title, *Worlds Beyond the World: The Fantastic Vision of William Morris*, I have discussed the origins of the English fantasy novel in the late nineteenth century. Tolkien begins with many of the formal and rhetorical precedents suggested by Morris, and contributes significant innovations of his own. His work is without parallel or precedent in its total coherence, and its lofty proportions and wide popularity show how mythic writing can function in an age which does not willingly believe in myth. Its concern with the spiritual questions of free will and pure heart in a world beset by loss and by desire for power add a different slant to the socialist-humanist philosophy Morris propounds through his fantasy. The two authors are equally concerned with philosophical ideas and with moral purposes; they are both projecting an heroic literature of alternatives, a literature directed toward community rather than individualism; but Tolkien fundamentally differs from Morris, whose hero could frankly admit, "Friend, I never saw a soul save in the body."

The highest reality for Morris was a bodily reality, a tangible, solid, human contact of brotherhood, fellowship, and physical attunement to nature. Tolkien's very image of creation—the music of the Ainur—and his symbol for moral or spiritual purity—the light which first streamed from the Two Trees and later was preserved only in the Silmarils—are not images with physical substance, but airy, intangible realities that cannot be held and touched unless corrupted (the imprisonment of the light in the Silmarils, for instance). The decline into mere substance is a fall—the substance of the Ring which must be destroyed, or the body of the Silmarils which allows them to be seized, giving rise to chaos and conflict. Tolkien has managed to convey a spiritual quality beyond the material plane. His image of the soul is not so much *in* the body, as streaming *out* of the body in the form of light or music or enchanting story.

Tolkien's formal achievements in literature will need to be assessed when his influence can be more clearly seen. It is doubtful that *The Silmarillion* will establish a pattern for others to create similar scriptural texts, but it may very well serve to revive some of the older texts his form is based upon. He is a fundamentally conservative writer, in the best sense. His conservatism is manifest in the return motif which reestablishes the old order at the end of *The Lord*, so that the new age of Men will be a continuation of the ancient kingdoms; it is evident in his adherence to the hierarchical and conservative Catholic religion; it is symbolically revealed in *The Silmarillion*, which is essentially an anti-Promethean book, advocating obedience and harmony, eschewing discord and rebellion. This places Tolkien at nearly an opposite pole from the radical Morris, who championed revolutionary politics and creative dissent in the body politic.

The Promethean archetype seems to run under and through the fabric of Tolkien's writing, and is one reason, perhaps, he made his hobbits into lovable thieves. The hobbit makes the Promethean urge look small and silly, and this is part of the purpose of anti-heroic central figures. The gigantic forces of evil Bilbo and Frodo face have all stolen power by force. The hobbits, small and folksy burglars, on the other hand, trivialize acts of thievery. They gain their ultimate victories in spite of their tendency to burgle—though Frodo must sacrifice a finger in the process. Sam's temptation to take the Ring is another point at which the Promethean possibility is considered and rejected in nearly comic terms. But the real Promethean rebellion, to which all the episodes in *The Hobbit* and *The Lord* refer, is fully described in *The Silmarillion*.

Tolkien substitutes light for Promethean fire, and Melkor/Morgoth is the negative Prometheus, ruler of the Orcs. It is no accident that the race of slaves to the Dark Lord should have the same name as the symbolic hero of William Blake's *America* (also appearing in other Blakean prophecies). According to

Northrop Frye, "Orc is the power of the human desire to achieve a better world which produces revolution and foreshadows the apocalypse." He describes him as a "giant or devil living in what to the orthodox is Orcus or Hell," and he explains that "Orc, then, is not only Blake's Prometheus but his Adonis, the dying and reviving god of his mythology." Tolkien is a far more orthodox Christian than Blake or Morris: he mirrors death and resurrection in his pure and faithful characters and accords ultimate destruction to dark forces. He accepts the Northern view of courage only within temporal limits, for he ultimately believes the forces of light will win and the old order—God's order—will be renewed.

Despite the fact that Tolkien's fiction is prompted by deep and traditional religious impulses, the tales curiously lack an overwhelming Divinity. He may be said to have written the closest thing to an epic since Milton, but it is an epic with a thoroughly anti-heroic set of heroes—where the hero could not have been heroic alone. When Frodo turns thief at the end, the very treachery which leads the fallen hobbit Gollum to bite the Ring from Frodo's hand and tumble into the Crack of Doom is a nearly comic rendering of the Fortunate Fall, with the beastly and possessive side of our nature paradoxically bringing us to the purification by burning which is a preface to renewal. Even Gandalf is clearly fallible and vulnerable; he is exceptional, but not divine. It is a considerable accomplishment for Tolkien to have written this great tale of paradise, loss, and consolation within a strong Christian tradition, and neither fall into repetitious allegory nor clever detachment.

No intervening God, but the ordinary working of creation fulfills the renewal in Tolkien's myths. This is the great task Men face, and the importance of the Great Project is one of the messages conveyed in Tolkien's own great project of *The Silmarillion*—it is what gives order and significance to the other elements of his subcreation, and has analogies with life and history, religion and morals, language and myth. When the vision of such a Project is awakened, the ordinary man, Tolkien says, is capable of great deeds. The world is full of extraordinary things, challenges which we are all capable of rising to and meeting, though we may not think we are. Tolkien calls his readers to high purpose, and in *The Silmarillion*, which is obviously the work of a scholar, he calls us to high learning as well. He elevates our conception of our capabilities, reminds us of the influence of language upon thought, and gives us varied testimony of faith in the larger order all these potentials mirror.

Finally, part of Tolkien's achievement, like Milton's, is his ability to express himself in a personal way through this vast, potentially impersonal narrative. He achieves an intimacy improbable in epic. We sense his human instincts as father, friend, and even as a slightly tongue-in-cheek professor; effects which probably wouldn't have developed had Tolkien gone straight on with *The Silmarillion* first and not detoured into his other fine books. Tolkien's restraint in not rendering a commanding God, the range of his fiction from children's story to Bible, and his skill at achieving human intimacy in the macrocosmic tale, are further reasons for the success of his fantasy. He has achieved the "elvish craft" he describes in his essay "On Fairy-Stories"—'living, realized sub-creative art. . . wholly different from the greed for self-centered power which is the mark of the mere Magician.'

SELECTED CRITICAL SOURCES

Biography

Humphrey Carpenter, *Tolkien: A Biography* (Boston: Houghton Mifflin, 1977).
Daniel Grotta-Kurska, *J. R. R. Tolkien: Architect of Middle Earth* (New York: Warner Books, 1976).

Criticism

Randel Helms, *Tolkien's World* (Boston: Houghton Mifflin, 1974).
Clyde Kilby, *Tolkien and The Silmarillion* (Berkhamsted, England: Lion Publishing, 1977).
Paul H. Kocher, *Master of Middle Earth: The Fiction of J. R. R. Tolkien* (Boston: Houghton Mifflin, 1972).
William Ready, *Understanding Tolkien and The Lord of the Rings* (New York: Warner Books, 1968) [Originally titled *The Tolkien Relation*].
J. R. R. Tolkien, *The Tolkien Reader* (New York: Ballantine, 1966) [contains "On Fairy-Stories"].

BIOGRAPHY & BIBLIOGRAPHY

JOHN RONALD REUEL TOLKIEN was born January 3, 1891, in Bloemfontein, Orange Free State, in what is now South Africa. His father, Arthur Reuel Tolkien, was a bank teller, and died suddenly three years later. With the death of his mother, Mabel (Suffield) Tolkien, Ronald was left an orphan. He attended King Edward VII School in Birmingham, and later obtained his B.A. and M.A at Exeter College, Oxford University. Tolkien was Rawlingson and Bosworth Professor of Anglo-Saxon at Oxford from 1925-1945, and Merton Professor of English Language and Literature from 1945 to his retirement in 1959. Tolkien married Edith Mary Bratt on March 22, 1916 (she died in 1971); they had four children, John Francis Joseph Reuel (born 1917), Michael Hilary Reuel (born 1921), Christopher John Reuel (born 1924), and Priscilla Mary Reuel (born 1929). He died in Bournemouth, England, while visiting friends, on September 2, 1973. A list of his fantasies follows:

1. *The Hobbit; or, There and Back Again*. George Allen & Unwin, London, 1937, 310p, Cloth, Novel
2. *Farmer Giles of Ham*. George Allen & Unwin, London, 1949, 78p, Cloth, Story
3. *The Fellowship of the Ring*. George Allen & Unwin, London, 1954, 423p, Cloth, Novel [Lord of the Rings #1]
4. *The Two Towers*. George Allen & Unwin, London, 1954, 352p, Cloth, Novel [Lord of the Rings #2]
5. *The Return of the King*. George Allen & Unwin, London, 1955, 416p, Cloth, Novel [Lord of the Rings #3]
6. *Tree and Leaf*. George Allen & Unwin, London, 1964, 92p, Paper, Coll.
7. *The Tolkien Reader*. Ballantine, New York, 1966, 288p, Paper, Coll.
8. *The Road Goes Ever On; a Song Cycle*. George Allen & Unwin, London, 1967, 62p, Cloth, Songs [music by Donald Swann]
9. *Smith of Wootton Major*. George Allen & Unwin, London, 1967, 62p, Cloth, Story
10. *The Lord of the Rings*. George Allen & Unwin, London, 1968, 1077p, Paper, Novel [the first edition in one volume]
11. *The Silmarillion*. Houghton Mifflin, Boston, 1977, 365p, Cloth, Coll. [edited by Christopher Tolkien]

THE MILFORD SERIES:
Popular Writers of Today

To order, please send price plus 50¢ for postage and handling to The Borgo Press, P.O. Box 2845, San Bernardino, CA 92406. California residents please add 6% sales tax. Write for our free catalog of books in print. CIP.